HOW TO
THINK
LIKE AN
ENTREPRENEUR

By the same author:

How to Think Like Sherlock
How to Think Like Steve Jobs
How to Think Like Mandela
How to Think Like Einstein
How to Think Like Churchill
How to Think Like Bill Gates
How to Think Like da Vinci
How to Think Like Stephen Hawking
How to Think Like Sigmund Freud
How to Think Like Barack Obama

HOW TO THINK LIKE AN ENTREPRENEUR

DANIEL SMITH

Michael O'Mara Books Limited

First published in Great Britain in 2020 by
Michael O'Mara Books Limited
9 Lion Yard
Tremadoc Road
London SW4 7NQ

A CIP catalogue record for this book is available from the British Library.

Papers used by Michael O'Mara Books Limited are natural, recyclable
products made from wood grown in sustainable forests. The manufacturing
processes conform to the environmental regulations of the country of origin.

ISBN: 978-1-78929-207-7 in hardback print format
ISBN: 978-1-78929-241-1 in trade paperback print format
ISBN: 978-1-78929-208-4 in ebook format

1 3 5 7 9 10 8 6 4 2

Designed and typeset by Envy Design Ltd
Printed and bound by CPI Group (UK) Ltd, Croydon, CR0 4YY

www.mombooks.com

For Charlotte and Ben – get to business!

Contents

Contents

Introduction

Entrepreneur *n*. a person who undertakes
an enterprise or business, with the chance of
profit or loss.

THE CONCISE OXFORD DICTIONARY

'The entrepreneur always searches for change,
responds to it, and exploits it as an opportunity.'

PETER DRUCKER, *THE DAILY DRUCKER* (2004)

Entrepreneurs have been with us throughout history. There was, I expect, some cave dweller who realized they were a dab hand at roasting a bit of bison and so set up a little enterprise swapping dinner for raw meat, or a container of water or a lovely wall painting. But it is only in more recent times that *entrepreneur* has entered the popular lexicon and has come to be acknowledged as a vital component of our economic systems.

In the early days of formal economic study – dating back to the Enlightenment or thereabouts – there was an assumption that economic actors (i.e. people!) were rational creatures who made reasoned decisions based on an analysis of all the evidence available to them. There was little room in that model for the notion of entrepreneurs, who tend to be individuals prepared to act both instinctively and in a risky manner, choosing an uncertain path in the hope of rich reward. But from the mid-twentieth century there was a greater understanding that much economic activity is not conducted on the basis of cool, calm rationalism

– and this realization has allowed the figure of the entrepreneur to come to the fore.

So, what exactly do we mean when we talk of entrepreneurship? When broken down, it is a relatively simple concept. The entrepreneur is an individual who creates a business to fill a gap in the market, shouldering the large part of the risk and consequently enjoying the majority of any resulting rewards. Typically, the entrepreneur is also an innovator, employing new ideas to fulfil the consumer's demands. Joseph Schumpeter (1883–1950) was among the first economists to truly celebrate such figures and the dynamic disequilibrium they bring to the market, which he considered the sign of a healthy economy.

Unlike those in professions such as law or medicine, the entrepreneur does not have the comfort of a defined path to travel. Their journey is intrinsically perilous, dotted with numerous obstacles and a constant threat of ambush. In a 2014 article for *Forbes*, Steve Blank – a veteran of numerous start-ups since the 1970s – gave a taste of that uncertainty: 'The safest bet about your new business is that you're wrong... A start-up is not about executing a series of knowns. Most start-ups are facing a series of unknowns – unknown customer segments, unknown customer needs, unknown product feature set, etc.' Ultimately, the entrepreneur must be able not merely to cope but to positively flourish as they find their own path. Inevitably, hard work tends to be part of the deal, so learning quickly and working smart are vital skills too. As Roy Ash, former director of the US Office of Management and Budget, put it in 1984: 'An entrepreneur tends to bite off a little more than he can chew hoping he'll quickly learn how to chew it.'

This book, I hope, will help you to get into the psychology of the entrepreneur as we consider the challenges they face – from first having an innovative idea to ultimately marshalling a fully fledged business. We will see that the journey requires passion, courage, self-belief and initiative as well as level-headedness, resilience, flexibility and much else besides. We will explore the psychology behind crucial tasks such as branding, hiring and scaling up. Even more fundamentally, we will look at how leading entrepreneurs broke free of the niggling doubt that 'I can't do this' to discover that 'Yes, I can'. As Sunil Mittal, head of the vast Indian-based Bharti Enterprises, told Knowledge@Wharton in 2008 about his own early days in business: 'That defiance of the conventional wisdom, to my mind, was very important – and being determined to challenge that thought that you can't do it as a young entrepreneur.'

When reading this book, it is worth remembering that the entrepreneurs whose thoughts, ideas and experiences are explored should not necessarily be regarded as models of all that is good in humanity. Very few have demanded to be put on a pedestal or to be considered as role models outside of the commercial sphere. Many will have had their run-ins with the authorities at one time or another. Perhaps they have violated competition rules or employed questionable systems of labour. Even as I was finishing this book, one prominent entrepreneur was acquitted of defaming an innocent third party after a trial that, despite his acquittal, could hardly be described as edifying. Their presence in these pages is not to promote worship of them as heroes, but rather because, regardless of any particular foibles, they are successful business figures who have had interesting things to say or demonstrate about the art of entrepreneurism.

That said, we will also see that it is possible to be a hard-nosed business success and maintain a core of basic decency. Take Richard Branson's observation in Martyn Lewis's 1997 book, *Reflections on Success*:

> I think that people have the idea of an entre-preneur being the sort of stereotype person who treads all over everybody and bullies their way to the top. There certainly are people like that, and they have managed to get away with it, but they generally get their comeuppance in the end.

Indeed, there is plentiful evidence contained herein that entrepreneurism and making the world a better place are far from mutually exclusive – whether it's the philanthropy of the Silicon Valley mega-rich set, or the sort of principled business dealing championed by the likes of Anita Roddick. She was a woman who perfectly encapsulated her own theory of what an entrepreneur should be like: 'An entrepreneur is very enthusiastic and dances to a different drumbeat, but never considers success as something which equates to personal wealth.'

I shall leave the last word with Amazon founder Jeff Bezos, who told Inc.com in 2004: 'Entrepreneurship is really more about a state of mind than it is about working for yourself. It's about being resourceful. It's about problem-solving.'

Spot Your Gap
in the Market

'Opportunities are like buses – there's always
another one coming.'

RICHARD BRANSON, 2012

The job of the entrepreneur is theoretically very simple. Spot a gap in the market and fill it. Sometimes, it might be the case that you provide a good or service that no one else is offering. Other times, there may be existing providers but you work out a way to provide the good or service better or more cheaply, so winning customers to your enterprise and away from your rivals.

When considering what market gaps you might fill, the following questions are worth considering:

- What are you good at? Entrepreneurs have been known to set up businesses in areas where they have spotted a gap but lacked personal expertise. But if you choose to do so, you will need to surround yourself from the outset with people who can make up for the shortfalls in your knowledge and experience. Most entrepreneurs prefer to focus on areas that have some personal resonance. Silicon Valley, for instance, is filled with many more tech-geeks than tech-phobes!

Spot Your Gap in the Market

- Is your chosen market missing a trick? Is innovation your gift? In 2008, for example, Travis Kalanick and Garrett Camp were leaving a conference in Paris when they were unable to hail a cab. They realized that there now existed mobile-phone technology that could revolutionize the process of ordering and tracking cabs – and so Uber was born.
- Or are you about perfecting what already exists? Could you replicate what other businesses are already doing but better? Can you provide a level of customer service that the established businesses are failing to meet? Are you destined to found the bakery that serves up the tastiest bread, or open the fashion boutique stocking the best lines in the business?
- Can you gauge the demand? Your idea might be the product of genius but is the market big enough to sustain a new entrant? Is your offering distinct enough that the existing players won't simply be able to respond and shut you out?

Key to establishing the gap you are going to fill is openness. The greatest entrepreneurs are flexible thinkers, in terms of considering both what aspects of a market are failing and how those failures may be rectified. As Michael Dell, the founder of Dell Computers, has noted: 'It's through curiosity and looking at opportunities in new ways that we've always mapped our path.' Dell enjoyed its own period of heavy growth in the 1990s and into the new century by recognizing a market gap – a growing number of tech-savvy individuals keen to buy customized computers direct from the manufacturer for delivery within just a few days. No one else was concertedly meeting the demand, so Dell stepped in and reaped the rewards.

There are also two distinct methods of gap-spotting. Sometimes, the entrepreneur actively steps up to search out the gap, while others find the gap discovers them. A prime example of the first is Jack Ma, founder of the Alibaba Group. He realized that his native China was not taking advantage of the opportunities offered by the exponential growth of the internet when he set up his business in the late 1990s. He took it upon himself to step in to fill the shortfall, building a web platform to connect Chinese businesses into the global network. Moreover, Ma proves that you don't necessarily need deep expertise to succeed in a given market. He is an internet billionaire who claims to have written barely a line of code in his life!

Larry Page and Sergey Brin, meanwhile, can be placed in the second category. In the mid-1990s the pair were studying at Stanford, working with algorithms in a bid to achieve better internet search results. They started assembling a vast collection of internet links with their doctoral dissertations in mind, and had no intention of building anything so grand as a search engine. But before they knew it, that was where their work had led them. 'Then we told our friends about it and our professors,' Page explained to *Bloomberg Businessweek* in 2004. 'Pretty soon, about 10,000 people a day were using it. We realized by talking to all the CEOs of search companies… that commercially, no one was going to develop search engines. They said, "Oh, we don't really care about our search engine." And we realized there was a huge business opportunity and that nobody else was going to work on it.'

The really great entrepreneurs keep on seeing new gaps even as they succeed in filling an old one. Netflix, for example, is a business that has reinvented itself to fill a range of evolving gaps in the entertainment industry. Back in 1997 its founders, Reed Hastings and Marc Rudolph, realized that consumers were beginning to consume entertainment in a different way. Where people might once have gone to their local Blockbuster store to hire a video, customers were now growing used to online retailers like Amazon. Netflix thus started out as a DVD-rental service, taking orders online and dispatching discs through the post. But, as the years went by, a new phenomenon took hold – that of streaming content online direct to personal devices. Netflix turned its back on its old, dying model and reinvented itself: first as a downloadable service and then as a streaming service. More recently, as other players have entered the streaming-service market,

Netflix has also become a content producer, investing huge sums in a bid to be one of the foremost providers of original content.

Talking to *Wired* in 2012, Hastings gave an eloquent expression of the inherent risks involved in attempting to spot the gap in a market and determining to be the one to fill it: 'But as an entrepreneur you have to feel like you can jump out of an aeroplane because you're confident that you'll catch a bird flying by. It's an act of stupidity, and most entrepreneurs go splat because the bird doesn't come by, but a few times it does.'

Back Yourself

'The way to get started is to quit talking and
begin doing.'

WALT DISNEY (ATTRIB.)

Many millions of people around the world dream of being their own boss, of running their own business, of making a successful enterprise out of a great idea they've had. Yet only a small minority even get as far as giving it a go. Instead, they stick to what they know, working for other people, often exploiting their own talents to help make a fortune for someone else. The first characteristic a successful entrepreneur needs is self-belief. If you do not believe you have what it takes to succeed, you can be sure that no one else will. Without the confidence to take a step into the unknown – to build a business all of your own – your dreams will remain just that: the unrealized contents of your mind.

All successful entrepreneurs share in common that moment of decision when they pledged to themselves to translate their ideas into action. They each decided that they would back themselves to succeed in the marketplace, even when the safer option might have been to take a regular job and let someone else take all the risk. They opted to shoulder the risk themselves, optimistic that they could do things well enough to reap the accompanying rewards. They listened to the inner voice that told them: 'You can do this.' In a commencement address he gave at Stanford University in 2005, Apple co-founder Steve Jobs spoke on the subject of following your own path:

Your time is limited, so don't waste it living someone else's life. Don't be trapped by dogma – which is living with the results of other people's thinking. Don't let the noise of other's opinions drown out your own inner voice. And most important, have the courage to follow your heart and intuition. They somehow already know what you truly want to become. Everything else is secondary.

Some aspiring entrepreneurs are held back by the fear that their business idea is not yet fully formed. While no one can expect to make a success of a business with a half-baked scheme, it is also true that very few enterprises come to life with all the ingredients already in place to guarantee success. The chances of having a product or service, a brand, marketing, finance and market contacts all in place from day one are remote indeed. A vital component of the entrepreneurial journey is allowing yourself the time to build your business and get it ready for customers. Aiming for your business to be the best that it realistically can be from the off is admirable; believing it can be perfect is folly. As Facebook's Mark Zuckerberg told *Wired* in 2016: 'If you believe something must be fully perfect just to get started, a lot of the time you'll never get started.'

The legendary fashion designer Coco Chanel offers a good case study in the importance of an entrepreneur having faith in themselves as their No. 1 asset. Her start in 1883 as Gabrielle Bonheur Chanel was a humble one. She was the illegitimate daughter of a laundrywoman and street hawker, and her mother died when she was just twelve years old. She then spent the next few years in a convent where she learned to sew, using this valuable skill to get work as a seamstress. But few anticipated that she would amount to anything much.

However, Coco sensed that there was change in the air. She had started her career altering clothes so that women could achieve the desired silhouette of the day by cramming their bodies into corsets and adorning their dresses with unwieldy bustles. But by the 1910s she had a growing sense that for the first time there was a significant number of women expecting an existence outside of the domestic setting. Coco's customers were now eager for clothes that looked good but were practical and comfortable too. And she decided she was the woman to provide them.

She secured seed capital to open a small millinery shop in Paris, then another in the coastal town of

Deauville and a third in Biarritz. She was a creative marketer, paying a couple of young, good-looking relatives to parade around Deauville in her clothes. By 1918, she had raised enough money to open her first full fashion boutique in the heart of Paris's fashion district, earning a worldwide reputation and a personal fortune for her always elegant but also practical fashion lines for women, employing innovative new materials like jersey fabric to cater for a new market of liberated women.

She serves as a blueprint for self-starters everywhere. It would have been easy for her to conclude that people like her, from backgrounds such as hers, simply did not run their own multinational businesses (the barriers to market in the early part of the twentieth century were, needless to say, comparatively much higher for women than they were for men); but she backed her own skills as a designer and also as a business brain to become an international business icon. Following that Disney mantra, she did not settle for talking and instead set about doing.

A SPANKINGLY GOOD IDEA

Another entrepreneur who had the courage to build her business even when the market seemed to be telling her not to try was Sara Blakely, the founder of underwear-manufacturer Spanx, Inc. Blakely had the idea for her trademark body-shaping footless pantyhose when she was working as a sales trainer in the scorching heat of Florida. She wanted the benefits of pantyhose but restyled to suit her preference for open-toed sandals. She invested her life savings in developing a prototype but her business idea was rejected by every hosiery-maker she approached – some even suggesting that her concept was so outrageous that it must be a prank. But eventually one mill-owner asked his daughters what they thought of the idea and when they said they liked it, he agreed to begin manufacture. The Spanx brand proved a huge hit and Blakely joined the ranks of self-made billionaires.

Inspiration and Perspiration

'The critical ingredient is getting off your butt and doing something.'

NOLAN BUSHNELL, FOUNDER OF ATARI AND CHUCK E. CHEESE, CITED BY CHUCK GALLOZZI ON TOPACHIEVEMENT.COM

All entrepreneurs are to a lesser or greater extent dreamers but it is the ability to use your dreams and ambitions as a spur to action that turns someone from merely a dreamer into an entrepreneur. As Bushnell put it in an extension of the above quotation: 'It's as simple as that. A lot of people have ideas, but there are few who decide to do something about them now. Not tomorrow. Not next week. But today. The true entrepreneur is a doer, not a dreamer.'

It is a sentiment echoed by entrepreneurs from throughout the ages. Thomas Edison put it as well as anyone when in 1923 he noted to members of the press: 'None of my inventions came by accident. I see a worthwhile need to be met and I make trial after trial until it comes. What it boils down to is 1 per cent inspiration and 99 per cent perspiration.' Edison was a bona fide genius yet he was at pains to suggest that you can have the biggest dreams and best ideas, but they will count for little if you are not prepared to put in the hard work to make them a reality.

Inspiration and Perspiration

'Colonel' Harland David Sanders, founder of Kentucky Fried Chicken, was another whose entrepreneurial success was in large part down to his extraordinary work ethic. He laboured variously on the railways, as a ferryman, as a travelling salesman and as a gas-station attendant on his way to business success. At one stage, he even used his private living quarters adjacent to the first restaurant he established to provide space for an overflow of customers. Meanwhile, when not serving those customers, he spent his free time perfecting his frying techniques and developing the 'secret recipe' coating that would ultimately earn him his fortune.

More recently, Bill Gates has revealed that he did not take a single day off in his twenties as he strived to establish Microsoft as the world's leading software company. Similarly, Jeff Bezos was known for working twelve-hour days, seven days a week during Amazon's infancy, often rising at two or three in the morning to make sure orders were shipped on time. His work ethic was already evident at school, with one former fellow student ruefully recalling that when Bezos declared his intention to be high-school valedictorian, all the other students accepted that they would be vying for second place. Then there is Indra Nooyi, former CEO of PepsiCo, who worked midnight until 5 a.m. as a receptionist to put herself through Yale and who later declared in an interview that she used to wish there were thirty-five hours in the day in order to get more work done.

Another who put in the long hours was Gary Vaynerchuk, growing his family wine business from a $3 million concern to a $460 million one in his first five years as boss. In his 2009 book, *Crush It! Why Now Is the Time to Cash In on Your Passion*, he summed up his recipe for success: 'Love your family, work super hard, live your passion.'

But what if the equation that more hours = more success is flawed? Plenty of people think it is. That is why the notion of 'working smarter, not harder' has gained so much leverage in recent years. Its advocates argue that offices full of zombified, demotivated workers who have forgotten why they came to work in the first place really do not propel a business forward. Instead, progress is made by alert workers who have the personal resources and energy to strategize their 'to do' lists and focus on those tasks that will most impact the business. The so-called Pareto principle, for example, suggests that 80 per cent of business is generated by 20 per cent of leads. Imagine the gains to be made by someone working smart to strategically identify which 20 per cent of leads to focus on against the energy-sapping work of doing the rounds in the vague hope of turning up a client.

Smart working also requires people to examine their individual strengths and weaknesses, allowing them to go full-throttle on what they're best at and to share out those tasks that play less to their strengths. An entrepreneur may think that they are maximizing their chances of success by putting 110 per cent of their energies into their business. But, as every schoolkid knows, it is not humanly possible to put in that level of effort anyway – and even if it were, your stocks of energy would soon be burned up and you burned out.

In 2013, Meredith Fineman – founder of FinePoint, a communications and professional-development company – took on the subject of smarter working in an article for the *Harvard Business Review*:

Just because you clocked 15 hours at your office, with likely dry eyeballs and a complete lack of focus, doesn't mean you've accomplished things in a smart way. Many people have written or spoken about this. Typically, you have 90–120 minutes before you devolve into internet fodder or social media. If you're putting in 15 straight hours at your desk, without breaks, how good is your output? How much time are you wasting?[...]The distinction between working hard versus smart has hit me as an entrepreneur [...] This isn't to say you shouldn't be diligent or that you should half-heartedly execute, but rather, that it's crucial to know what you have to do as opposed to everything you could do. It's about being strategic.

Richard Branson is among the most high-profile advocates of greater flexibility in work patterns. His company, for instance, offers work-from-home options as well as unlimited leave. The idea is not that employees work less but that by helping people achieve a better balance between their professional and private lives, they will be happier and more productive – to everybody's advantage. Technology raises the prospect that in the future workers might be able to achieve as much in three or four days as they do in a full week now. 'Everyone would welcome more time to spend with their loved ones, more time to get fit and healthy, more time to explore the world.' Branson says his wager is that by worrying less about how long they have to spend in the office, his labour force will work smarter. (Although it is worth noting that there is evidence to suggest an unlimited leave entitlement actually results in some employees taking less leave in a bid to keep their bosses happy. The road to hell, as they say, is paved with good intentions.)

Hard work is, of course, a vital component in any successful enterprise. But hard work for the sake of it is pointless. The successful entrepreneur is a doer but one who seeks out those tasks they can complete to positive advantage. In the words of billionaire investor Warren Buffett: 'I don't look to jump over seven-foot bars: I look for one-foot bars that I can step over.'

Dream Big…

'All of us need a vision for our lives [...] Success comes when you surrender to that dream – and let it lead you to the next best place.'

OPRAH WINFREY, *O,*

THE OPRAH MAGAZINE (2001)

Every entrepreneur's adventure starts with a dream – an idea that they can use their talents to build a business. To be a success, an entrepreneur needs to be many things: practical, a self-starter, strategic, sensible, ambitious, realistic, to name just a few of the necessary attributes. What an entrepreneur does *not* need to be is delusory, foolish, chasing after a half-baked fantasy. The trick is to avoid becoming a fantasist but to hang on to that initial dream. Of course, the entrepreneur should not sacrifice their business on the altar of the unachievable. But they should also avoid becoming shackled by fear of failure.

Of the current generation of entrepreneurial giants, surely none is a bigger dreamer than Elon Musk. Here, after all, is a man who has his head not merely in the clouds but deep into outer space. He has a track record of developing ideas that might seem wholly unrealistic to most of us, but which he approaches with a practical zeal to turn them into reality. As Bill Gates has noted: 'There's no shortage of people with a vision for the future. What makes Elon exceptional is his ability to make his dreams come true.'

By Musk's own admission, not all of his schemes work out as he plans, but plenty do. As such, his career is an object lesson in how seemingly outrageous dreams and wily entrepreneurship can co-exist. Even for those entrepreneurs operating in far more 'down-to-earth' sectors (which, let's be honest, is most of them!), Musk still provides valuable lessons. It is sometimes said that politics is the art of the possible, but much the same can be said of entrepreneurship. Something may seem impossible, a step too far, but the truly ambitious entrepreneur should be wary of discarding a dream without first investigating whether it could be brought to fruition after all. As he told *Esquire Magazine* in 2012: 'The first step is to establish that something is possible; then probability will occur.'

Musk permitted himself to dream from his earliest days. He was studying for a doctorate in the mid-1990s when he realized that the internet was going to shape the world. He dreamed of being part of it but the stakes were high, as he could have stuck to the path he was on that would no doubt have brought him a good level of success and security of itself. 'That summer of '95,' he told *Who's Time*, a Chinese financial show, in 2014, 'it seemed to me like the internet was going to have a big effect on humanity. I thought, "Well, I can either work on electric vehicle technology and do my

PhD at Stanford and watch the internet get built or I could put my studies on hold and try to be part of the internet.'" Musk, as we all know, chose the latter. First he founded PayPal, which he sold for close to $1.5 billion in 2002. Subsequently, he became a senior figure at Tesla Motors, a forward-looking motor manufacturer specializing in electric cars as well as renewable energy. But it is perhaps his role in the space transportation company SpaceX that best epitomises Musk, the dreamer with a plan. As the company's founder and leading light, he has been integral to the pursuit of practical solutions that might yet make previously unimaginable intergalactic exploits achievable. Here is a company that has a stated aim, for example, of cutting the cost of space transportation with a view to eventually colonizing Mars. In 2015, Musk told the International Space Station Research & Development Conference: 'If SpaceX and other companies can lower the cost of transport to orbit and perhaps beyond, then there is a lot of potential for entrepreneurship at the destination.' This is nothing less than science fantasy turned into hard-nosed entrepreneurism.

Ask virtually any successful entrepreneur the secret to their success, and you'll be hard-pressed to find one who says they won through by putting a cap on their dreams (even if they employ a series of checks and balances to ensure that their dream is rooted in the possible). Take, for example, Oprah Winfrey, quoted at the start of this chapter, and ever the advocate of chasing the big dream. 'Playing small doesn't serve me,' she told *Fortune* magazine in 2010. 'The truth is, I want millions of people. I'm not one of those people who says, "Oh, if I change just one person's life..." Nope, not satisfied with just a few. I want millions of people.' And millions she has touched, but the harnessing of that ambition was possible only by allowing her ambition the space to breathe in the first place.

Meanwhile, Google has become a crucial part of our everyday lives. It is increasingly difficult to imagine what life was like before its creation. Yet, when Sergey Brin and Larry Page started out, the idea of designing a search engine with the global reach of Google seemed about as wild as Musk's aspirations to people Mars. As Larry Page remembered in a commencement address he gave at the University of Michigan in 2009:

I have a story about following dreams [...] it's a story about finding a path to make those dreams real [...] Well, I had one of those dreams when I was 23. When I suddenly woke up, I was thinking: What if we could download the whole Web, and just keep the links, and [...] I grabbed a pen and started writing! [...] Amazingly, I had not thought of building a search engine [...] When a really great dream shows up, grab it!

It can be intimidating to hear such advice from the modern masters of commerce. Easy for them, we might think, to say 'Hold on to your dreams' when their dreams were turned into multibillion-dollar corporations. But for every Winfrey, Musk and Page there are myriad lower-profile entrepreneurs who followed a similar path: daring to dream and turning the dream into reality. The scale of a dream is in any case a qualitative rather than quantitative matter. Musk's big dream is mastery of the universe. That is the right fit for him. Someone else's big dream might be to own a single shop or to run an online business from their bedroom. The point is, each entrepreneur owes it to themselves to allow their personal dream to grow as big as it can.

In Barry Farber's *Diamond Power: Gems of Wisdom from America's Greatest Marketer* (2003), the controversial but always quotable self-help guru Napoleon Hill observed the following: 'Cherish your visions and your dreams as they are the children of your soul, the blueprints of your ultimate achievements.' The image is a powerful one, all the more so when taken with another of his observations, this time concerned with turning aspiration into reality: 'A goal is a dream with a deadline.'

... But Start Small

'Even if your ambitions are huge, start slow, start small, build gradually, build smart.'

GARY VAYNERCHUK, *CRUSH IT! WHY NOW IS THE TIME TO CASH IN ON YOUR PASSION* (2009)

While ambition is a prerequisite for entrepreneurial success, it is worth keeping in mind that no business comes into the world as a fully formed success. All of them start as the kernel of an idea in somebody's mind. In other words, they all start small. As Lao Tzu, the great strategist and philosopher of Chinese antiquity, put it in the *Tao Te Ching*: 'A journey of a thousand miles begins with a single step.'

Every enterprise's rate of progress is different; letting your business grow organically from small beginnings does not represent lack of ambition. Perhaps the big break will come after a month, six months, six years – as long as your business is developing in the right direction and continues to work for you, don't be tempted to rush it along before it is ready. It's always better not to run before you can walk. By all means take the opportunity to push your business forward, should it arise (see page 92), but do be wary of forcing the issue when the opportunity is not yet there.

There is another old saying, sometimes attributed

to Robert Louis Stevenson: 'Don't judge each day by the harvest you reap, but by the seeds you plant.' This is great advice for the entrepreneur in the early stages of their journey. Of course, it is great to have a bulging order book and an expanding bank balance at the earliest opportunity. But even if your business is not booming (and as long as it's not sending you catastrophically into the red), it might be laying down all the roots that will eventually result in that bloom of success. Are you providing a good or service the market wants? Can you supply it at a sensible price, for both you and the consumer? Do you have at least the makings of a customer base prepared to spend their money with you again? Is your brand getting out there and known? These are all signs that you are planting those seeds successfully, so don't race ahead of yourself.

Take the case of Facebook. Here is a thoroughly modern business that seemed to come out of nowhere and take over the world in a blink of an eye. In 2004, Mark Zuckerberg – then a twenty-year-old student at Harvard University – launched thefacebook.com from his dorm room. Inspired by the tradition of college yearbooks in which students' information (like mini-biographies and contact details) was included, he set up his website as a means by which his fellow students at Harvard could connect. After he had signed up somewhere near half the student body, he then thought about further expansion. Over the next few months, he rolled it out to other colleges and universities throughout the country. Zuckerberg was careful to take it one step at a time, making sure his market existed and that his website did what it needed to.

Within ten months, Facebook had a million users. Within two years, that figure had grown to 50 million, and hurtled towards a billion by 2012. Today, Facebook has something in the region of 2.5 billion users. It is a huge company that has expanded exponentially, but Zuckerberg was sensible enough to let this happen at its own pace. He had the patience to start small and evolve the business from there. As he told a 2012 Startup School hosted by the seed accelerator Y Combinator: 'I think it took a year for us to get 1 million users and we thought that was incredibly fast. And I think it is, but it wasn't as quick as a lot of things grow today. And I think actually having that time to bake it was really valuable for us.' Now, not every entrepreneur is going to achieve (or even necessarily want) Facebook-levels of commercial success. Growth for most will be a smaller-scale, slower process but it is instructive that even the corporate giants go through a stage of infancy.

Google followed a similar pattern, with founders Larry Page and Sergey Brin birthing the company in a garage, starting small before growing it into the business with a market capitalization value that eclipses even Facebook's. Consider also the case of two childhood friends, Ben Cohen and Jerry Greenfield. In 1977 they took a correspondence course in ice-cream making and the following year opened up an ice-cream parlour called Ben & Jerry's in what was once a gas station in Burlington, Vermont. They waited until 1981 until their first franchise branch opened, and by 2000 the company was a global brand with a reputation for ethical trading. It was then that the founders sold the business to international conglomerate Unilever for in excess of $300 million. Go back even further, and you find that John Pemberton – a veteran of the US Civil War – established the global Coca-Cola empire from a single soda fountain in a drugstore in Georgia, where he had developed a 'French Wine Coca' to act as a nerve tonic.

All of these entrepreneurs followed a strategy for new businesses that was summed up by the self-help author Napoleon Hill in his *The Law of Success: In Sixteen Lessons* (1928): 'If you cannot do great things, do small things in a great way.' At a time when their businesses were too young and underdeveloped to be the commercial giants they would become, they each nurtured their enterprises and made sure that what they could do was done exceptionally well. Then, when the time was ripe for growth and development, they were ready for it.

Being an entrepreneur is a bit like parenting. You want your child to grow big and strong, to be able to stand on their own two feet, to be independent and durable. But it's a long game, and no parent expects their child to be ready to take on the world the moment you get them home from the delivery suite. Nor should the long-term entrepreneur expect their business to go into overdrive from the moment they first open the shop doors. 'The secret of getting ahead,' Mark Twain is rumoured to have said, 'is getting started. The secret of getting started is breaking your complex, overwhelming tasks into small manageable tasks, and then starting on the first one.' Or as T. E. Lawrence says in the movie *Lawrence of Arabia*: 'Big things have small beginnings.'

Have a Plan

'In preparing for battle, I have always found that
plans are useless but planning is indispensable.'

DWIGHT EISENHOWER, AS QUOTED BY

RICHARD NIXON (1962)

There is a story about a woodsman that is often attributed to Abraham Lincoln (but which in truth likely first appeared in C. R. Jaccard's 1956 article 'Objectives and Philosophy of Public Affairs Education'). The woodsman, it is told, was once asked, 'What would you do if you had just five minutes to chop down a tree?' Mulling the question for a while, he responds: 'I would spend the first two and a half minutes sharpening my axe.' The moral of the story: preparation is vital to success.

For proof of such an obvious statement of truth, one need only watch an episode of *The Apprentice* or some such similar show to realize that even some of the supposedly brightest entrepreneurial minds sometimes forget the importance of planning altogether. And it rarely plays out well.

All too often, entrepreneurs new to the scene fail to carry out the due diligence on their business aspirations. An idea strikes and in the ensuing excitement it is too easy to keep putting off the business plan until another time… which inevitably never comes. Before you know it, there is a business with premises and significant capital investment and still no one has sat down with a blank sheet of paper to work out a) whether the business has a realistic chance of success, and b) what the business might look like in a month, a year, or five years. But even in the bedlam and excitement of starting a new enterprise, it really is worth taking the time out to think it all through. As Warren Buffett said in 1991 (quoted in Andrew Kilpatrick's *Of Permanent Value: The Story of Warren Buffett*, 2007): 'Someone's sitting in the shade today because someone planted a tree a long time ago.'

What then is the purpose of a business plan? Here are just a few of the benefits:

- To strength-test your business idea.
- To clearly define your vision for the business and what it is for.
- To acknowledge your organization's strengths and weaknesses.
- To establish the values by which you will operate.
- To give a realistic appraisal of your likely expenses, revenues and profits.
- To serve as a sanity check when the going inevitably gets tough.
- To set targets and goals.

- To provide analysis of the market and your competitors.
- To focus in on who your customers are and how you can serve them.
- To guide your marketing strategy.
- To inform your recruitment process.

Once you have a robust plan, you can also then share it with others. A viable business plan is generally a prerequisite for bank financing, and any responsible investor is likely to demand one too. If someone is happy to throw money at you without a real sense of how you intend to use it, they are probably not the sort of investor you want on board. Even if you turn to friends and loved ones for capital, it is only fair (and a way of avoiding recriminations further down the line) to ensure that everyone is aware of what the overarching ambitions for the business are. That way, if things start going off track, it is easier to identify what is going wrong, what might be corrected and what is perhaps, after all, an unviable proposition.

If everyone buys into the plan from day one, then it is much less likely that any one individual will shoulder the blame for failure should the plan have been broadly followed. More optimistically, it also allows everyone a greater buy-in when success comes calling. A strong business plan can help get your business's new employees up to speed, too, by introducing them to your culture and expectations (although it is generally advisable to keep the financial minutiae to yourself).

It is important to keep in mind, however, that while your plan should serve as a roadmap for your business, it should also be flexible enough to deal with changing circumstances and unforeseen challenges. Far too many of us have submitted financial forecasts to bosses knowing that everyone involved is only too aware that the figures have been derived from hopeful speculations and, occasionally, wild guesses. In truth, no one *knows* what is likely to happen in five years, least of all economically. As the US economist and Stanford professor Ezra Solomon once noted: 'The only function of economic forecasting is to make astrology look respectable.' Similarly, Warren Buffett has suggested most economic forecasts say more about the forecaster than reality. 'I don't read economic forecasts,' he told *Businessweek* in 1999. 'I don't read the funny papers.'

Amazon founder Jeff Bezos is another who cautions against over-reliance on a business plan. *Forbes* quoted him thus: 'Any business plan won't survive its first encounter with reality. The reality will always be different. It will never be the plan.' But Bezos is not saying that planning for your business is a waste of time. It is safe to say that Amazon's success is not the result of its founder making decisions on the hoof without some overarching vision for the company's future in mind. Instead, Bezos is pointing out that sticking rigidly to a plan even as you become aware of new information and unexpected circumstances can be as damaging as having no plan at all. (See the following chapter for more on the benefits of adaptability.) As he explained to *Foreign Affairs* in 2015:

> You can't sit down to write a business plan and say you're going to build a multibillion-dollar corporation; that's unrealistic. A good entrepreneur has a business idea that they can make work at a much more reasonable scale and then they proceed adaptively from there, depending on what happens.

The entrepreneur should not regard their business plan as an unbreakable declaration of how they expect the future to play out. Instead, it should serve as a way to prepare them and their business for whatever the future might hold – based on the best available evidence but also informed by the knowledge that you cannot possibly have taken account of everything. No business plan can guarantee you a trouble-free ride to success but it might just stop you from tripping over your own shoelaces. As the Reverend H. K. Williams famously observed in a 1919 edition of *The Biblical World*: 'Remember, if you fail to prepare you are preparing to fail.'

SHORT AND SWEET

Airbnb founder Brian Chesky is a great advocate of keeping your business plan simple. Interviewed for Fast Company in 2014, he revealed that he sketched out the company's entire business strategy for that year on a single piece of paper – a document he referred to as 'The infamous paper to take over the world!' 'When you have too many initiatives,' he said, 'it's really hard to keep your focus,' adding: 'If you can't fit it on a page, you're not simplifying it enough.'

Be Adaptable

'There's just one thing that's permanent in this world, and that's change.'

HENRY FORD, IN AN INTERVIEW WITH BRUCE
BARTON, 'IT WOULD BE FUN TO START OVER
AGAIN', *THE AMERICAN MAGAZINE* (1921)

While it pays to have a plan, adaptability is also an essential trait of successful entrepreneurship. No matter how much careful planning you put into your business, the nature of commerce is such that you are always at the mercy of circumstances beyond your control. You might run the best ski chalet in the world, but that's no consolation if all the snow melts in time for the season. Or perhaps you have the best little coffee shop in town, but who cares if the coffee harvest failed and you can't get hold of the beans you need? Or if your chief barista resigns on order to go and retrain as a Buddhist monk somewhere in deepest Nepal?

That's when you need to show that you're not a one-trick pony but a business chameleon, changing to suit your environment and adapting as the component parts of your business move and alter. Perhaps you can convert your ski chalet into a private spa for the season, and that coffee shop could corner the market in speciality teas instead. Some ideas may pay off and some might fall by the wayside. But the sure-fire way to failure is inaction when things start going off-piste. As Richard Branson wrote on his blog in 2008: 'The best, most solid way out of a crisis in a changing market is through experiment and adaptation.'

When it comes to adaptability, the small start-up entrepreneur often finds themselves at an advantage over their larger, more-established competitors. Giants commonly dominate a stable marketplace, using their size to outmuscle the competition. But when conditions change, giants find it a lot harder to reposition themselves. So it is that even when market disruption might seem like an unwelcome distraction for the small-scale entrepreneur looking to stick to their business plan as best they can, it might actually be a chance to make up some ground on their competitors. No less a figure than Mark Zuckerberg (who, let's remember, started his empire from his college dorm room) went on record to *Businessweek* in 2012, saying: 'I would like Facebook to always operate as fast as a company that's ten times smaller than we are.' In other words, when the time comes that you need to act quickly and adapt to changing circumstances, better to be lean and hungry than big and cumbersome. It is an idea Zuckerberg had explored with chat-show host Charlie Rose a year earlier when he talked about the advantages of being a business focused on one or two core activities rather than one of those corporations 'trying to do everything themselves'. 'And we just believe,' Zuckerberg said, 'that an independent entrepreneur will always beat a division of a big company...' Similarly, Sunil Mittal lays a good deal of credit for his early success with his ability to move quicker than his larger opponents. He told the 2008 US–India Business Council's annual meeting in Washington, D.C.:

If you're caught between speed and perfection, always choose speed, and perfection will follow. You never wait for perfect positioning, because in business you don't have the time; especially if you're small, you can't do it [...] And the large companies took their own time. They were months behind us, and that made us pick up a market niche for ourselves, which in turn made us big.

So, how does having a plan fit in with being permanently adaptable? The two are by no means mutually incompatible. Indeed, an entrepreneur is far more likely to be able to respond in a prompt and strategic way if they have an overriding scheme to guide them. To put it another way, it is very much easier to go off-plan when you have a plan to go off! Here are a few useful guidelines to ensure that your business remains flexible and tenacious whatever circumstances you face:

- Take the broad view. It might be the case that you are integral to your business in a day-to-day, hands-on sort of way. You might be a one-person band, doing it all. Regardless, if you are the boss of your business, you need to find a way to take yourself out of the minutiae and get an overview. Buy in some help if need be but give yourself the time and space to look at the big picture and think long term and strategically.

- Keep cool. It's easy to get caught up in the emotion of the struggle when your business faces challenges. But a cool head is essential in order to respond to challenges appropriately and adapt the way you do business. Keep an eye on your bottom line. However committed you are to your business vision, don't fall into the trap of pursuing it at any cost. Temper your vision to stave off disaster. Then you can take the time to regroup, learn from your experience and reset your business on a better footing.

- Create a culture of robustness and adaptability. You set the tone for your business, so strive to ensure that your staff feel comfortable dealing with the curveballs that will inevitably come their way. Remember, too, that your staff might be the first to detect the rumblings of a potential crisis or changing circumstances. They may get a sense of what is happening in the marketplace earlier than the boss, who may be several steps removed from it. Make sure they know that you want to hear about potential problems and that, between you, you will find a way to deal with them. As Mark Zuckerberg commented at Y Combinator's Startup School in 2013: 'One definition that I have for a good team is a group of people that makes better decisions as a whole than they would individually make.'

- Keep your eyes and ears open. The best time to start preparing for things going wrong is when things are going right. Don't get complacent in the good times but instead survey the entire market; look at what's going on with your rivals and at what's happening in the world in general – be alert to even the subtlest clues that things might be about to change. Don't wait until that snow doesn't arrive or the coffee crop has already failed; keep an eye on the weather reports and prepare a plan for how you can adapt if the worst happens.

- Always be ready to learn. The most adaptable people have the most adaptable brains. The moment you think you know it all is the moment you will struggle when the unexpected happens. Always be willing to learn from others, whether from an experienced mentor, a customer or the newest face in your workforce. Great ideas can come from anywhere and they may just help you dig yourself out of a hole.

- Adapt from a position of strength. When things are going well, it is easy to get lulled into thinking that you have worked out how to play the game. But the most successful entrepreneurs are not those who stick to a winning formula but those who change things up and reinvent themselves. Follow the example of Thomas Edison, often considered the greatest inventor to ever come out of the USA. He was also a business genius, establishing enterprises across an array of sectors. Adaptability was one of his watchwords, and he invested heavily in research and development to ensure he was always one step ahead of the game. When a new employee joined his company in 1903, he asked Edison what laboratory rules he wanted him to observe. 'Hell!' Edison shot back. 'There ain't no rules around here! We are tryin' to accomplish somep'n!'

- Adaptability is not the same as panic. Adaptation is about being strong, so don't turn your business into a reed that bends with the breeze. Consider what change is necessary, and what change stems from a knee-jerk response to the unexpected. Consider Jeff Bezos's observation to the *New York Times* in 2002: 'The mistake that companies make is that when the external world changes suddenly, they can lose confidence and chase the newest wave.'

STRAIGHT TO DUPONT

The US conglomerate DuPont provides a neat case study in the advantages of adaptability. Founded in Delaware, USA, in 1802 as an explosives manufacturer, it provided some 60 per cent of the Union Army's gunpowder during the US Civil War. But when peace descended, the company drew on its expertise to adapt and branch out, becoming a market leader in the production of, for example, synthetic rubber, polymers (like polyester, nylon and Teflon), agricultural products, healthcare products and electronics. Then, in 2017, it merged with Dow Chemical in a deal worth well over $100 billion as it prepared to meet the new challenges of an ever-changing global chemicals market.

There is much to be said for the values of consistency and reliability when it comes to business. But these things should never come at the expense of being able to react and adapt. Adaptation, after all, is a hallmark of humankind's success in the world. Consider the words of Leon C. Megginson, a management sociologist at Louisiana State University, who in 1963 wrote an article entitled 'Lessons from Europe for American Business' (published in *Southwestern Social Science Quarterly*). Megginson paraphrased the teachings of the great naturalist and founding father of the theory of natural selection, Charles Darwin, for his business-minded audience: 'It is not the strongest of the species that survives, nor the most intelligent, but rather the one most adaptable to change.'

Turn Obstacles into Opportunities

'The knowledge that you have emerged
wiser and stronger from setbacks means that you
are, ever after, secure in your ability to survive [...]
Such knowledge is a true gift, for all that it is
painfully won.'

J. K. ROWLING, HARVARD COMMENCEMENT
ADDRESS (2008)

Resilience is a necessary requirement for any entrepreneur, wherever they may be in their career. But you can be sure you'll need it in abundance in the early stages of establishing your business. The pay-off is that if you can successfully weather the problems and jump over the hurdles you'll inevitably face, you'll emerge all the stronger and wiser. As General Custer is said to have once uttered, 'It's not how many times you get knocked down; it's how many times you get back up.' It is an adage that stands up as much for people in commerce as for soldiers or sportsmen.

Take the case of Henry Ford. When the American car-manufacturing business ran into serious problems in the years following the 2008 global financial crisis, many commentators wondered what Ford would have made of it all. It was him, after all, who had transformed the industry at the turn of the twentieth century. Before him, motoring was an elitist hobby but, thanks in large part to his perfecting of the industrial production line, he made the car an object for the masses. The

Turn Obstacles into Opportunities

Ford Motor Company's Model T sold in excess of 15 million vehicles, earned Ford a fortune and changed the face of transport history. Yet only two years before he established his eponymous company, Ford declared himself bankrupt after the failure of his previous motoring business, the Detroit Automobile Company. It had produced only some twenty cars in the two years of its existence as Ford struggled to find a design and production process that worked. Other less driven characters might have given up at that stage, but not Ford. He took on board the lessons of this ill-starred venture and soon established a new, sleeker company fit to dominate the marketplace. Within a decade he was not only outrageously rich but a behemoth of the industrial world for the ages too.

The ability to roll with the punches, learn from setbacks and accept them as a natural part of growth and development has in recent years been couched in terms of a 'growth mindset'. Carol Dweck popularized the concept in her 2006 book, *Mindset: The New Psychology of Success*. She wrote:

> In a growth mindset, people believe that their most basic abilities can be developed through dedication and hard work – brains and talent are just the starting point. This view creates a love of learning and a resilience that is essential for great accomplishment.

By embracing hard work and perseverance, she argues, it is possible to learn more and faster, especially when challenges and failure are regarded not as impediments to success but as opportunities to learn and improve.

There are few more striking recent examples of the uber-resilient entrepreneur than Oprah Winfrey, who has overcome a litany of challenges in both her personal and professional life. Her story is ultimately one of self-empowerment, in which personal development and self-knowledge have gone hand in hand with professional success. Overcoming a multitude of challenges has been crucial to her evolution. 'Ever notice how some of the most eye-opening moments in life occur when the going gets tough?' she told *O*, her own magazine, in 2014. 'Rough patches are scary, for sure, but they can also be truly transformative.'

Today she counts as a global icon who has evolved from a broadcaster and actor (one who was up for an Oscar for her performance in *The Colour Purple*) into the boss of a vast media, entertainment and business empire. In 2019, Forbes estimated her net worth at a cool $2.7 billion. But she has had more than her fair share of those 'rough patches' she mentioned.

When she was born to a teenaged single mother in rural Mississippi in 1954, there seemed little prospect of her achieving such extraordinary success. Her early years were marked by acute poverty and she also survived sexual abuse. Pregnant by the age of fourteen, she prematurely gave birth to a son who died in infancy. She next went to live in Tennessee and, despite being a young black woman in the American South as it was engaged in a fierce battle with the civil rights movement, she began to turn her life around. She took responsibility for her own life ('[...] we all are responsible for ourselves [...] You cannot blame apartheid, your parents, your circumstances, because you are not your circumstances. You are your possibilities. If you know that, you can do anything,' she told *O* in 2007) and determined that she would use all her experiences, both good and bad, to propel herself forward. 'I know for sure that all of our hurdles have meaning,' she wrote in her 2014 book, *What I Know for Sure*. 'And being open to learning from those challenges is the difference between succeeding and getting stuck.'

A job in local radio, landed while she was still at school, led to a role as a news anchor and, then, a chat-show host. Her natural skills as a communicator ensured a growing audience share, which prompted her decision to launch her own production company. By the age of thirty-two, Winfrey was a millionaire and within a decade she had found a place on the Forbes 400 with a fortune of \$340 million. By 2003, she was the world's first self-made black female billionaire. Throughout, she has pushed herself to tackle new challenges, unafraid to fail. 'Do the one thing you think you cannot do,' she told *Forbes* in 2012. 'Fail at it. Try again. Do better the second time. The only people who never tumble are those who never mount the high wire.'

In *What I Know for Sure*, Winfrey likened life's challenges to earth tremors. Those tremors are, she suggested, an unavoidable facet of human existence. And the only way to endure them is to change your stance so they don't knock you down for good. 'But,' she said, 'I believe these experiences are gifts that force us to step to the right or left in search of a new centre of gravity. Don't fight them. Let them help you adjust your footing.'

In other words, even as a tremor may leave you shaken and perhaps even feeling broken, let it serve as a guide. 'Your life is your greatest teacher,' she said in an interview at Stanford Graduate School of Business in 2014. 'Every single thing that's happening to you every day; your joys, your sadnesses, your challenges, your worries [...] Everything is trying to take you home to yourself. And when you're at home with yourself [...] you are your best.'

It is a sentiment with which Richard Branson concurs. Talking to Success.com in 2009, he declared: 'The challenge is to follow through on great ideas. I think if [you've] got a great idea, you need to just give it a try. And if you fall flat on your face, pick yourself up and try again. Learn from your mistakes.'

THE GENESIS OF AN INTERNET MARVEL

The Chinese e-commerce company Alibaba is among the largest corporations in the world. The experiences of its founder, Jack Ma, are an object lesson in resilience and perseverance. In the mid-1990s he was an English teacher visiting the US when he had his first taste of the internet. Up until that time, he had endured many professional disappointments. He twice failed his university entrance exams and was rejected from Harvard's business school no less than ten times. In fact, when the first Kentucky Fried Chicken franchise came to China, they rejected him for a job there too. But Ma does not lack self-belief. 'Never give up' is a life motto. His trip to America left him wondering how the internet might serve the particular needs of the Chinese market. He set up Alibaba in 1999 but success didn't come at once. There was much trial and error before he got the business model right and for a few years survival was the company watchword. But by 2015 *Forbes* ranked Ma among the world's twenty-two most powerful people. 'The incessant effort and constant ability to learn from our mistakes led to success,' he said in 2004. 'While today is tough, tomorrow can be even tougher. However, the day after tomorrow may be beautiful. But too many will give up after tough times on the eve of tomorrow night. Therefore, never give up today!'

Perfect Your Offering

'Good design is good business.'

THOMAS WATSON JR, PRESIDENT OF IBM,
IN AN ADDRESS AT THE UNIVERSITY OF
PENNSYLVANIA (1973)

Elite sportspeople often speak of the tiny margins between success and failure, and the few fractions of a percentage point that separate the good from the very best. It is the difference between an Olympic champion and an also-ran, a World Cup footballer and the player forever warming the bench. So too in the world of entrepreneurism, where competition is routinely fierce and the demand for better is constant.

In such circumstances, it is vital that the entrepreneur ensures that what they offer to the market – whether a good or a service – is the absolute best that it can be. A customer may return to a favourite restaurant for years on end but it can take just one bad meal to ensure they never set foot in the establishment again. The highest standards must not only be set but maintained too.

Arguably, no one better understood this than Steve Jobs at Apple, where he fostered a culture that melded together cutting-edge technology with an artist's sense of the aesthetic. Apple became one of the world's largest companies by seamlessly blending together science, functionality and beautiful design. It was perhaps Jobs's grasp of this latter aspect that truly set him and his products apart. Other companies could rival Apple for technical innovation and for ease of use but few if any came close to competing with the sheer finesse that the company brought to products like the iPod, iPad and iPhone. It was in his demand for faultless design that Jobs discovered those tiny margins that elevated his company to the ranks of the elite. In his own words: 'Design is not just what it looks like and feels like. Design is how it works.' And Apple's designs under his guidance routinely worked beautifully.

Delve back into history and we discover plenty of Jobs's spiritual forefathers, people who realized that commercial dominance relied on the perfecting of their offering. Take, for example, the exploits of Josiah Wedgwood, who in the eighteenth century built a business empire selling chinaware of a quality hitherto thought beyond Western manufacturers. 'I want to astonish the world all at once,' he claimed.

Wedgwood lived in England at a time when the Industrial Revolution was changing the face of society. The population was becoming more urbanized and the middle class was rapidly expanding. As a result, there was a surge in demand for fine chinaware, which previously had been the preserve of the rich upper class, who bought expensive porcelain sourced from China. The rest of the population, meanwhile, tended to make do with basic, low-grade chinaware produced by domestic factories.

Wedgwood, though, saw the commercial possibilities if he could somehow use the latest technical innovations to produce chinaware to rival the quality of that imported from China, which he could then sell at a lower price to the burgeoning new middle-class market. Wedgwood was a brilliant autodidact with a hunger for hard work. He taught himself entirely new methods of production, sourced the best-quality clays, invented new glazes and laboured over designs that would capture the collective imagination (and that remain extraordinarily popular to this day). Before long, he counted not only the aspirational middle classes but also royalty among his fans. Queen Charlotte, wife of George III, commissioned a tea service from him, while Catherine II of Russia was the beneficiary of a specially designed 952-piece dinner service. The following quote by Wedgwood (cited in *Elbert Hubbard's Scrap Book*, 1923) gives a taste of his perfectionist zeal and his belief that excellence is a commercial imperative:

Beautiful forms and compositions are not made by chance, nor can they ever, in any material, be made at small expense. A composition for cheapness and not excellence of workmanship is the most frequent and certain cause of the rapid decay and entire destruction of arts and manufacturers.

Such was his confidence in the quality of his merchandise that he is believed to have been the first major commercial figure to promise 'satisfaction guaranteed or your money back'.

From Wedgwood back to Jobs, then, whose approach echoed Wedgwood's in its pursuit of excellence. Part of Jobs's gift was to be able to spot those who could work to the exacting standards he demanded. While he didn't craft all of Apple's products with his own hand, he assembled the teams that did. Among them was the British designer Jonathan Ives, who at Jobs's funeral in 2011 spoke of his former boss's clamour for perfection. Ives recalled that Jobs would air all sorts of ideas at brainstorming meetings; and, while some were 'dopey' and even 'truly dreadful', others 'took the air from the room' and were 'bold, crazy, magnificent ideas, or quiet simple ones which, in their subtlety, their detail, were utterly profound'.

Ives made his name at Apple as a chief designer on the iMac, which, with its sensual triangular form and see-through casing, changed the way that people thought about personal computers. But he was also an integral part of the team that came up with the iconic design for the iPod a few years later. Like Jobs, Ives believed that design should not be about getting in the face of the user but should instead be characterized by simplicity and uncluttered elegance. The iPod brought together new technology (the ability to store a mass of songs in a tiny machine, and a hierarchical system of menus to search and select individual tracks), an elegant new tool for searching through menus (the revolutionary click-wheel that sat flush on the front of the device) and a series of stylistic innovations (from the thinner-than-a-pack-of-cards dimensions to the monochrome finish, and even details such as etching serial numbers into the iPod itself rather than having to use unsightly stickers).

It was another instant design classic straight from the Jobs production line. It is tempting to think that Apple at this time was permanently crackling with inspired genius. But Jobs worked his teams (sometimes mercilessly) in pursuit of the little bits of magic to elevate a product from good to classic. Ives has described the arduous processes of consultation and negotiation that took place between designers, engineers and manufacturers, which meant that every product was being constantly revised, changed and, ultimately, perfected.

Usain Bolt won all his Olympic golds because of the long, hard sessions he put in on the practice track even on the days when he'd rather have been putting his feet up at home. Similarly, Lionel Messi plays like the ball is glued to his foot because of the untold hours he spent honing his skills long before he ever stepped near Camp Nou. So too, the magic of the iMac, iPod and all those other Apple products were the result of hard, painful graft, as were Wedgwood's achievements centuries earlier. Virtually every premium product that comes to set the standards by which their rivals are judged – think design classics like the Bic ballpoint pen, Levi Strauss's denim jeans or the Lego bricks that captivate generation after generation – comes with a similar backstory of hard work and innovation by their creators. Being an entrepreneur is not all about working yourself into the ground. But the truly successful entrepreneur is the one who pushes themselves that bit further than feels comfortable to make sure that they are offering their customers the very best they could wish for.

Customer is King

'I make sure that I spend most of my time out
and about, talking to people, asking questions,
making notes, and experiencing my business
through customers' eyes.'

RICHARD BRANSON, *SCREW IT, LET'S DO IT:
LESSONS IN LIFE* (2006)

The everyday pressures of running a business can sometimes be such that you forget why it is you are doing it at all: to provide your customer base with the product or service they desire. Particularly if you are not in a customer-facing role, it is all too easy to lose sight of the people who ultimately pay your bills. But an entrepreneur does this at their peril. The moment that your customers cease to be front and centre of your thoughts is the moment your journey to commercial collapse begins. As Walmart founder Sam Walton once noted: 'There is only one boss. The customer. And he can fire everybody in the company from the chairman on down, simply by spending his money somewhere else.'

That is why the matter of understanding customers and their wants, needs and behaviour is itself a multibillion-dollar business. It is, though, possible to garner the most crucial customer information without paying a fortune for someone else to do it for you. As the Branson quote on the previous page suggests, the very best way is to speak directly to the people who are buying from you. What is it that they want from you? What are you doing well? What could be better? (And remember that, even if you think they are being unfair or unreasonable, the customer is always right – don't think of arguing the reverse, as that is the quickest way to ensure that they won't use your company again! Instead, listen to them and make them feel that their input truly matters. As Richard Branson told *Forbes* in 2016: 'A complaint is a chance to turn a customer into a lifelong friend. I say that seriously, not as some press-release baloney.')

Talking to staff is also a great way to get the low-down on what the customers think. It may be that the people on the shop floor (or its equivalent) get a more candid view of what consumers are really thinking than you as the boss will get in conversation. Consider using feedback forms too, and look at your raw business data. Which parts of your business are thriving and which are struggling? Ask yourself tough questions about why this may be. What do your customers look like? What makes them tick? Are they all a certain type of person? Why? How can your business adapt to appeal to a broader customer base?

History is littered with companies that forgot to put their customers first, especially when the customers' needs were changing. Take, for instance, Kodak, one of the giants of the photography business from its foundation in 1888. It was forced to file for bankruptcy in the USA in 2012, a victim of its slowness in realizing that customers were moving away from traditional film photography and striding confidently into the age of digital photography. Then compare Kodak's fate with the success of Beats Electronics. It was co-founded by hugely successful music producers Dr Dre and Jimmy Iovine in 2006, at a time when the headphone market was dominated by the sort of discreet earbuds then favoured by Apple. But Dre and Iovine were alert to the dissatisfaction that many customers had with this sort of product. At a time when vast amounts of money, energy and technological expertise were going into music production, many music fans wondered why they couldn't listen through equipment that fully exploited those high production values. Dre and Iovine listened and became convinced that there was a large market that would pay a premium for far higher-quality headphones than those then available. They were right – and in 2014 Apple, who were also listening to their customers, acquired the brand for in excess of $3 billion.

Go back further, and there is hardly a successful entrepreneur who made it without putting the customer first. At the beginning of the last century, for instance, Madam C. J. Walker earned a fortune by providing hair-care and cosmetics products specially designed to meet what had previously been the unmet needs of the large

African-American population. She opened her ears to those customers and reaped the rewards.

Perhaps the greatest cultivator of customer loyalty in the modern age has been Steve Jobs. He understood that his customers wanted sleek, beautiful and functional technology. But, more than that, he built his customers into a community, uniting them in the common belief that each of them was a creative freethinker in the mould of Jobs himself. You were either an 'Apple person' or you were not. But Jobs was not content simply to speak to his customers or rely on market research to guide what the company did. He believed that Apple should strive to inhabit the very same mental space as its customers. If Apple's designers and tech-wizards thought like their customers did, so the logic went, then they would be more likely to come up with the products that the customers wanted. In his own words, 'It's not about fooling people, and it's not about convincing people that they want something they don't. We figure out what we want. And I think we're pretty good at having the right discipline to think through whether a lot of other people are going to want it, too. That's what we get paid to do.' This is an attitude echoed by Jeff Bezos, who has noted: 'The best customer service is if the customer doesn't need to call you, doesn't need to talk to you. It just works.'

FASTER HORSES

There is an apocryphal story in which Henry Ford was asked about his innovations in the automotive industry and commented: 'If I had asked people what they wanted, they would have said faster horses.' Had it been left to the customer, he was suggesting, he might never have developed the motor cars that changed the world. Whether or not he actually said this, other great entrepreneurial visionaries have shared the view that listening to the customer ought not to be a block on innovation. Steve Jobs, as we have seen, accepted the customer as king, but not as head of product development. 'You can't just ask customers what they want and then try to give that to them,' he once said. 'By the time you get it built, they'll want something new.' Edwin Land, head of Polaroid, had made a similar point back in 1945: 'Very often the best way to find out whether something is worth making is to make it, distribute it, and then to see, after the product has been around a few years, whether it was worth the trouble.'

Regardless of the methodology, though, every entrepreneur needs to know who is going to buy from them, what they want, why they want it and how much they want to pay. By knowing the customer's expectations, it becomes possible to exceed them. It is then that the customer has good enough reason to buy from you and not from your competitors.

Embrace Rivalry

'A horse never runs so fast as when he has other
horses to catch up and outpace.'

OVID (43 BC – AD 17/18, ATTRIB.)

Jack Welch, head of General Electric for twenty years, used to say that when it comes to competition you should aim to 'buy them or bury them'. It's the sort of punchy adage that you might expect to be popular with entrepreneurs. Which aspiring magnate doesn't want to see their opposition crushed or at least brought under their control, clearing their path to market dominance? Commercial history is littered with great rivalries, where giants of their sectors slug it out to determine their respective shares of the spoils – think Coke and Pepsi, McDonald's and Burger King, VHS and Betamax, Apple and Microsoft. But is Welch's philosophy really the way forward?

As Ovid's quotation suggests, competition is best viewed not as an impediment to your success but as a spur to drive you on. Welcome competition, study it, see where the opposition excels and where they fall down, and then use that intelligence to inform your own business. Learn lessons from the competition so that you might become better than them. After all, competition is the underpinning tenet of the open markets that entrepreneurs inhabit. It encourages innovation, keeps prices low and stops monopolies rigging the market. Competition, to put it another way, keeps an entrepreneur honest, agile and on their toes. As Arie de Geus, head of Shell's Strategic Planning Group, told the *Harvard Business Review* in 1988: 'The ability to learn faster than your competitors may be the only sustainable competitive advantage.'

The trick is to learn quickly while not becoming fixated on the opposition. It is one thing to adapt your business to take account of your rivals and quite another to take the Welch approach of 'seek and destroy'. Ginni Rometty, IBM CEO, warned against such a trap in *Fortune* in 2014, commenting that, 'I believe the [...] thing is to never define yourself by competitors. You define yourself by either what your clients want or what you believe they'll need for the future. So: Define yourself by your client, not your competitor.'

Henry Ford, too, was wary of losing focus on what you are doing by looking too closely at what others are up to. He wrote in *Ford News* back in 1923: 'Competition whose motive is merely to compete, to drive some other fellow out, never carries very far. The competitor to be feared is one who never bothers about you at all, but goes on making his own business better all the time.' To never bother is, surely, a stage too far, but there is certainly a happy medium to be found. Perhaps retail magnate Harry Gordon Selfridge had it about right in his words cited in *Forbes Book of Quotations: 10,000 Thoughts on the Business of Life* (2016):

> Whenever I may be tempted to slack up and let the business run for awhile on its own impetus, I picture my competitor sitting at a desk in his opposition house, thinking and thinking with the most devilish intensity and clearness, and I ask myself what I can do to be prepared for his next brilliant move.

In other words, study your competition to generate self-awareness and self-improvement.

Jeff Bezos advocated a similar approach at the ShopSmart Shopping Summit in 2011, where he said: 'One way not to become complacent is to always have the beginner's mind. Have the mindset that you are the naïve one at this poker game, and there's probably somebody out there, unknown to you, who is doing a better job for the customer than you are.' He has also put into practice his long-held view that it is great to learn from the competition in private but folly to talk about them in public.

Appealing as it may sound in theory, the absence of any competition is generally a bad sign for the entrepreneur. To understand why, consider the three most likely reasons for a lack of rivals in your chosen field:

- You are ahead of the market. It is just possible that you have come upon a business idea to cater for a market that no one else has yet seen. This is the best-case scenario of the three options. It is also by far the least likely. The chances of you being first into an entirely new market are next to nil. And if you are by some chance first there, you may well be dealing with a market that is not yet mature enough to sustain your business anyway.
- Your market does not exist. Once smitten with a business proposition, it is easy to run away with the idea that everybody else will be too. 'Why has no one thought of this before?' you may well ask yourself. A vital secondary question must then be, 'Is it because no one actually wants what I plan to provide?' It is possible to create a market from nothing but it is extremely hard, especially for the lone entrepreneur. Absence of market is usually telling you that there is an absence of demand, so most likely it'll be back to the drawing board with your idea.
- You're not seeing the competition. It is natural to think that your business concept is unique, that your business is so 'one of a kind' that nobody will

be able to resist. But beware such self-delusion. Your cafe, say, may be unique in selling coffee brewed exclusively from beans passed through the digestive tract of a small tree-dwelling mammal. The coffee may even be truly delicious. You are absolutely convinced that any self-respecting coffee connoisseur will see you as the only place to go for refreshment. But to the majority of consumers, you will likely be just another coffee shop, and one whose drinks cost a lot more than the rivals. The cafe down the road selling mugs of instant coffee for a fifth of the price may well be the competition you aren't seeing.

Competition is the lifeblood of entrepreneurship. Take the rivalry that has existed for decades between fast-food giants McDonald's and Burger King. Both exist because there is a vast market for their offering and both emerged in the mid-1950s when changing lifestyles meant the market was mature enough to accept the 'fast-food' concept. To begin with, it seemed Burger King would lose out because it could not compete with its rival on price. But then it took a new, innovative approach, deciding instead to offer a bigger 'luxury' burger to sell at a premium price. The Whopper was born. Now it was the turn of McDonald's to pick up the gauntlet, so it set to work on developing a competitor to the Whopper, leading to the introduction of the Big Mac.

And so it went on: their competition informed the development of their menus, which in turn provided the consumer with more choice, which in turn propelled each company's expansion. Today, the market provides plentiful room for them both, and many other rivals besides, with competition continuing to force innovation (manifesting not least in the introduction of healthier options than the traditional burgers and fries, as well as vegan alternatives), which continues to spur demand, and so the wheel keeps on turning.

Then there is perhaps the greatest commercial rivalry of modern times, the gladiatorial contest between Bill Gates's Microsoft and Steve Jobs's Apple. It started in earnest in around 1983, when, with Microsoft set to unleash Windows on to the world, Jobs accused them of plundering the Mac's graphical interface. (Gates is said to have responded: 'I think it's more like we both had this rich neighbour named Xerox and I broke into his house to steal the TV set and found out that you had already stolen it.') The companies spent years in litigation over various disputes and the rivalry quickly escalated into a drawn-out slanging match between the two figureheads. Jobs, for example, suggested that Gates would have been a 'broader' guy 'if he had dropped acid once or gone off to an ashram when he was younger'. He also proclaimed: 'They [Microsoft] just have no taste. I don't mean that in a small way. I mean that in a big way, in the sense that they don't think of original ideas and they don't bring much culture into their products.' Gates, meanwhile, clearly annoyed, commented: 'If you just want to say, "Steve Jobs invented the world, and then the rest of us came along," that's fine.'

Yet when Jobs returned to Apple in 1997, Microsoft helped turn the company around by investing some $150 million in stock. The fates of the companies were far more intertwined than either man readily admitted, with each pushing the innovative envelope of the other over many years. By the time the two principals shared a stage in 2007 at the *Wall Street Journal*'s D: All Things Digital conference, much of the old vitriol had dissipated; and in 2011, when Jobs was nearing the end of his life, Gates visited him at his house and they spent many hours reminiscing. Their rivalry, despite being often spiky, had driven an extraordinary period of technological progress and was fundamental to creating a vast new global market. Both companies rank today among the most valuable in the world and it is difficult to think of a clearer example of the benefits of competition, not just for consumers but for the rival businesses themselves. As Gates (under)stated in 2008: 'Whether it's Google or Apple or free software, we've got some fantastic competitors and it keeps us on our toes.'

A SHOCKING AFFAIR

Back in the 1880s and '90s, Thomas Edison and George Westinghouse were the public faces of one of the great commercial rivalries of the nineteenth century. They fought to control the supply of electricity, each with a rival system – DC (or direct current) and AC (alternating current) respectively. Their contest became known as the War of the Currents. The tactics were often dirty, not least when the state of New York decided to adopt the electric chair as its means of executing criminals. Edison paid the chair's inventor to use Westinghouse's AC dynamos. He thus sought to build an association in the public's mind between his rival's current and its lethal application. In fact, he even attempted to popularize the expression 'Westinghoused' to describe someone who had been electrocuted!

Seize Your Moment

'Opportunities are like sunrises. If you wait too
long, you miss them.'

WILLIAM ARTHUR WARD, *FIRE-TONGUE* (1921)

In the movie *Dead Poet's Society*, Robin Williams plays John Keating, an English teacher at an elite boarding school in Vermont. He encourages his charges to follow their dreams, urging them: 'Carpe diem. Seize the day, boys. Make your lives extraordinary.' As for teenage boys, so too for entrepreneurs of whatever gender. Every successful business can trace its roots back to a moment where opportunity was seized. Many unsuccessful ones feature a sad story of opportunity missed.

One of the chief underlying causes of lost opportunity is a phenomenon often described as 'imposter syndrome' – a person's inability to believe themselves deserving of success on the basis of their own talents and effort. A great many entrepreneurs buy into this thinking. 'I am not ready,' they suppose. 'I need to know more/do more/have already proven myself. If I take my chance now, when I am unprepared, it is bound to fail. And then what?'

There is certainly much to be said for putting in the hard yards before opportunity comes knocking (see

Perfect Your Offering on page 69). But there is also a danger in over-preparedness. The art of entrepreneurship is by its nature full of risk. Minimize it as best you can, but do not get bogged down in the idea that you can bulletproof yourself from all danger. Get yourself to the stage where you know you can enter the market with a degree of confidence – but the gap in the market may disappear if you wait for your enterprise to be the finished article before you even start.

Besides, sometimes opportunity arrives when we least expect it. Someone like Ray Kroc (whose story is explored more fully on page 150) was well into middle age, in not particularly good health and stuck in something of a dead-end travelling-salesman role when he seized his unexpected opportunity. He turned a routine sales call into a life-changing moment as he realized that he had the vision to take the McDonald brothers' local burger-bar business and turn it into something far bigger. At a time when he was seemingly destined for an unremarkable end to an unremarkable career before retirement, he found that the planets had aligned and he eagerly grabbed his chance.

The unexpectedness of an opportunity ought never to count against it. It is rare that opportunity comes telegraphed far in advance. If you have a suntan lotion business, your business plan might be based on opening shop as soon as the summer arrives. But if there's an unexpected heatwave in early spring, only a fool (or the chronically underprepared) would let that opportunity drift. Sure, you might not have all aspects of your enterprise as ready as you would like given a few extra weeks. But if you can get your product to market and absorb some of the demand, you owe it to yourself to take the chance. Besides, if you do feel underprepared, you can console yourself with this thought from Richard Branson, which he has shared on Virgin.com: 'If somebody offers you an amazing opportunity but you are not sure you can do it, say yes – then learn how to do it later.'

This is an article of faith he has always lived by. In his childhood he earned the nickname Letsgo, while at Virgin he became known as Mr Yes. When he was the twenty-three-year-old boss of Virgin Records, Branson experienced one of those 'opportunity strikes' moments. At the time, he was concerned about the lack of headway one of his marquee signings, Mike Oldfield, was making into the US market. He had given Oldfield's *Tubular Bells* album to the head of Atlantic Records for a listen and it just so happened that it was playing in the office on the day that Atlantic received a visit from William Friedkin, who was seeking a suitable piece of music for his new movie, *The Exorcist*. *Tubular Bells* was put forward as a possibility, Friedkin liked it and Branson, as might be expected, said, 'Yes!' The film was one of the cinematic sensations of the decade, with the music a key element in building its atmosphere, and Oldfield was set on his path towards global superstardom – while Branson and Virgin enjoyed the secondary benefits of his huge record sales.

LEMONADE

What do you do if life gives you lemons? Make lemonade, or so says the old adage. So, what should you do if you're a jeweller and the diamond mines keep coughing up off-colour stones? Well, if you're the Le Vian company with a history dating back to the fifteenth century, you corner a new market. In 2000, the company registered the 'Chocolate Diamond' trademark and began a line of jewellery featuring brown diamonds of the sort traditionally reserved for industrial use. Despite initial scepticism from those who believe that a diamond should be flawlessly clear, the range took off. Le Vian had seized its moment and created a whole new classification of jewel.

Back in 2012, Sheryl Sandberg, Facebook's chief operating officer, shared her philosophy of seizing opportunity with graduating students from the Harvard Business School. 'If you're offered a seat on a rocket ship,' she urged them, 'don't ask what seat! Just get on.' She expanded on the subject in her 2013 book, *Lean In: Women, Work, and the Will to Lead*: 'There is no perfect fit when you're looking for the next big thing to do. You have to take opportunities and make an opportunity fit for you, rather than the other way around.' Addressing a female audience in particular, she noted: 'Women need to shift from thinking "I'm not ready to do that" to thinking "I want to do that – and I'll learn by doing it."' *Huffington Post* founder Arianna Huffington similarly encourages courageousness in taking on the challenges that opportunity presents. 'Fearlessness is like a muscle,' she tweeted in 2019. 'I know from my own life that the more I exercise it the more natural it becomes to not let my fears run me.'

Ted Williams is a baseball legend, the Boston Red Sox hitter acknowledged as one of the game's greats. In 1971 he published a book entitled *The Science of Hitting*, in which he described how the most important thing for a batsman is to wait for the right pitch. It is not a bad general rule for the entrepreneur: don't rush in, swinging wildly at the first opportunity that comes your way regardless of how good it is. But in baseball there is a rule that if you get three strikes you're out; thus a batter always has another chance to bat just around the corner. The entrepreneur might not be so lucky. Warren Buffett told an audience at British Columbia University in

2009: 'Don't pass up something that's attractive today because you think you will find something way more attractive tomorrow.' As most entrepreneurs will attest, 'the perfect opportunity' is a myth, so seize the merely promising one instead and work it with all you have. It is then that you can call upon the hard work you have already put in behind the scenes, in the hope that your business will stand as testament to the words of motor-racing legend Bobby Unser: 'Success is where preparation and opportunity meet.'

If at First You Don't Succeed…

'I made 5,127 prototypes of my vacuum before I got it right. There were 5,126 failures. But I learned from each one. That's how I came up with a solution.'

JAMES DYSON, *FAST COMPANY* (2007)

In our fast-moving world, there is a tendency to venerate success that appears to come quickly and effortlessly. 'Newer, younger, better' can seem to be the story that everyone wants to hear. But such thinking can be highly detrimental to the aspiring entrepreneur. Success can be fleeting, disappearing as quickly as it arrived. The truly great entrepreneurs are those who are in for the long haul. Sure, a few get lucky with their first big idea. But for most, the path to success takes a lot longer – and the experience garnered along the way can be vital in ensuring that their stay at the top is an enduring one.

Some of the greatest entrepreneurs the world has ever known encountered plenty of troughs before they reached their peaks. James Dyson – inventor, designer and multibillionaire founder of Dyson Appliances – is a prime example of one of those 'overnight successes' who actually took years to get there. In the late 1970s, he had an idea for a new type of vacuum cleaner that used new cyclonic vacuum technology to avoid the clogs that affected virtually every existing model on the market, so doing away with the need for expensive replacement bags. It was a great idea yet hardly anyone seemed interested – not least because there was a lot of money to be made by manufacturers forcing consumers to buy new bags for their vacuum cleaners every few weeks.

Undeterred, in the five years from 1979 until 1984, Dyson developed 5,127 prototype designs for his machine, each a little better than the last. Eventually, in 1985, a Japanese company licensed the new cleaner and it became a big hit there. Sales were sufficiently buoyant that six years later Dyson was at last able to start manufacturing the cleaner under his own company's name. He never looked back. But he also never forgot how all the low points helped define him and his company. Other hit innovations followed, including a revolutionary hand dryer that uses a thin sheet of moving air to remove water rather than evaporating it with heat, as well as hair dryers and hair curlers that incorporate similarly cutting-edge technology. He continues to invest billions in research and development, well aware of the need to have the courage and ambition to make a few missteps on the way to the great leaps forward.

In 2007, he told *Fast Company* magazine:

I don't mind failure. I've always thought that schoolchildren should be marked by the number of failures they've had. The child who tries strange things and experiences lots of failures to get there is probably more creative [...] We're taught to do things the right way. But if you want to discover something that other people haven't, you need to do things the wrong way. Initiate a failure by doing something that's very silly, unthinkable, naughty, dangerous. Watching why that fails can take you on a completely different path. It's exciting, actually.

Dyson is not alone in racking up failures on the path to success. Indeed, there are several notable cases where success came as a direct but unexpected result of failure. Take, for instance, bubble wrap. In 1960 two engineers by the names of Marc Chavannes and Al Fielding were trying to design a new type of textured wallpaper. Even as the fashions of the 1960s got wilder and more psychedelic, no one was particularly keen to cover their home with it. So, for a while, they tried to market it as a new type of housing insulation instead, but that didn't work either. Then some bright spark decided to use some of the bubble wrap to protect the latest IBM computer when it was being transported. Soon, bubble wrap became the wrapping of choice for millions of businesses and individuals who needed to send something precious from one place to another. Bubble wrap failed in what it was initially designed to do but that failure ultimately led to a much bigger commercial success than either Chavannes or Fielding could have imagined.

The life-saving compact pacemaker is another creation that emerged from serendipitous failure, in this instance after Wilson Greatbach accidentally put an incorrectly sized resistor into the electrical circuit of a heart-rhythm recording machine. Then there is WD-40 – the answer to countless household problems – which was given the '40' attribute because its inventors had worked through thirty-nine unsuccessful formulations before hitting their commercial home-run. Even the great Steve Jobs had his misadventures, being effectively forced out of Apple in 1985 after the relative lack of initial commercial success for the 'Lisa' and 'Macintosh' models. As history records, he returned to the company twelve years later to oversee the creation of a roster of products (the iPad, iPod and iPhone) that changed the face of technology and secured Apple's position as the biggest company on the planet.

The lesson for the budding entrepreneur is simple. Success rarely comes quickly. Often, it will arrive unexpectedly, or when you feel you are nearing the end of the road. But don't be put off by an initial lack of success. Hang on in there and keep working the right way, learning from your failures and missteps. It might turn out that they are not failures at all, so much as prototype models for your future successes. As Thomas Edison, industrial genius, is said to have uttered: 'I have not failed. I've just found 10,000 ways that won't work.'

Don't Fear Managed Risk

'A ship in harbour is safe, but that is not
what ships are built for.'

WILLIAM G. T. SHEDD, NINETEENTH-CENTURY
THEOLOGIAN (ATTRIB.)

Business is by its nature risky. Entrepreneurs invest time, effort and money with no guarantee that they will receive a return on that investment. Every entrepreneur, then, is a risk-taker. Needless to say, the idea is that they do everything within their power to diminish the risk of failure, but it can never be ruled out. You might have put in all the groundwork to ensure the success of your enterprise, only for everything to go wrong because of some set of unforeseen circumstances. It could be a natural disaster, a bout of serious illness, a change in regulations or the emergence of a new technology that renders your business defunct. Or something else entirely.

Risk is inevitable. The trick is to manage it. Sometimes, the budding entrepreneur decodes this advice as doing what they can to avoid it altogether. But for a business to grow and prosper, the more sensible route to take is to expose yourself to sensible, manageable risk. Success may not be guaranteed, but is there a reasonable chance that it might follow? Equally important, if it doesn't, can you weather the results of your failed gamble? If the answer to this latter question is yes, the wiliest entrepreneur might well decide their best course of action is to take on the risk in the reasonable hope of enjoying the rewards. In her commencement address at Johns Hopkins University in 2014, Susan Wojcicki, CEO of YouTube, put it like this:

> Life doesn't always present you with the perfect opportunity at the perfect time. Opportunities come when you least expect them, or when you're not ready for them. Rarely are opportunities presented to you in the perfect way, in a nice little box with a yellow bow on top […] Opportunities, the good ones, they're messy and confusing and hard to recognize. They're risky. They challenge you.

There is an episode from the very early days of Microsoft that neatly demonstrates how managed risk-taking can pay off for the budding entrepreneur. It was 1975 and Paul Allen, the company's co-founder alongside Bill Gates, read an article about the imminent release of the Altair 8800, a microcomputer developed by a New Mexico-based company called MITS. It was a pretty basic device but Allen suggested to Gates that they team up to write a language for it. So, Micro-soft (as it then was called) was born.

Gates, armed with only a company name and a burning desire not to miss out on what he and Allen sensed was a coming software revolution, approached MITS' founder, Ed Roberts. As unheralded entrants into the IT sector, Gates boldly claimed that his company had developed an interpreter that would allow the 8800 to run programmes written in BASIC – Beginner's All-purpose Symbolic Instruction Code, a computer language in popular use since the mid-1960s. This would vastly increase the potential use of the machine and Roberts's interest was duly piqued. Come to the offices in Albuquerque, New Mexico, six weeks later, he told Gates, to demonstrate the interpreter.

Gates had got a first foothold into the industry. But there was a problem. Micro-soft did not actually have an interpreter, nor an 8800 or the cash to buy one. Gates had taken an enormous risk by promising that which he did not yet have. If he could not come up with the goods, his nascent company would be a laughing stock, surrendering any reserves of credibility and goodwill before they had even got started. But Gates considered this a risk worth taking, confident that he and Allen would find a way to deliver. He secured access to the mainframe computer at Harvard's Aiken Computer Center and rigged up a simulation of the 8800 from information garnered from a magazine article. Working at a formidable intensity, they did indeed come up with a working interpreter in the available timeframe. 'It was the coolest programme I ever wrote,' Gates said about the project, according to James Wallace and Jim Erickson in their 1992 book, *Hard Drive*.

As events played out, it was Allen who went to the meeting to demonstrate it, and he was refining aspects of it all the way on his journey to the office. MITS were suitably impressed and bought up the system, launching Micro-soft (soon after to lose the hyphen) on their way to global domination. Gates had played a risky hand but one where he considered the odds to be sufficiently in his favour. And he was right. Howard Stevenson, a professor at Harvard Business School, has written on the theme of entrepreneurs who seek – as Gates did – to meet market demand even before they are in possession of the necessary resources. Indeed, he has described entrepreneurship as 'the pursuit of opportunity beyond resources controlled'.

Jeff Bezos was another willing to take risks at a young age. In 1994, having recently graduated, he looked set for life as a youthful senior vice president of a Wall Street hedge fund. But then he decided to play the odds, resigning his job to establish an online book retailer from his garage. The rest, as they say, is history, and today Bezos stands as the richest individual in the world. He had made a simple calculation: play it safe and wonder what might have been, or give his ambitions a go. 'For me,' he has said, 'I had to project myself forward to age 80. I don't want to be 80 years old, cataloguing a bunch of major regrets of my life.'

And still he runs his company on a system of managed risk, introducing innovations in the hope that they expand his business but aware that they might not. At the Bezos Code Conference in 2016 he spoke of his disappointment in the way that so many businesses (especially large ones) 'give up on things too soon'. At the Vanity Fair New Establishment Summit the same year, he argued that companies should be nimble and robust so as to 'be able to take a punch' and 'innovative and [do] new things at high speed'. Being prepared to take such risks, he argued, is 'the best defence against the future'.

All the statistics show that entrepreneurism is a high-risk undertaking. For example, US Census Bureau data reveal that, across all sectors, 55 per cent of new ventures die within the first five years. Of the remaining 45 per cent, 35 per cent fail during the next five. But where would the world be if everyone decided such odds are too intimidating? Entrepreneurs must be bold enough to take the risk and wise enough to minimize it. If you want to climb Mount Everest, you don't get up one morning, put on your hiking boots and a couple of extra layers of clothing and then head out hoping for the best. You need to have put in the hard graft beforehand, learning the skills, speaking to those who have already done it, making sure you have all the right equipment. Then you listen to the weather reports, waiting for just the right moment to set out. It's possible you still won't make it to the summit, but you've managed the risk and there's a reasonable chance you'll succeed. And, as Mark Zuckerberg pointed out in 2011: 'The biggest risk is not taking any risk [...] In a world that's changing really quickly, the only strategy that is guaranteed to fail is not taking risks.'

THE SPIN OF A WHEEL

While a good entrepreneur manages risk, it is generally not a great idea to base your business on the spin of a wheel, the toss of a dice or the turn of a card. However, that is just what FedEx founder Fred Smith did when his company found itself down to its last few thousand dollars in its early days. He took $5,000 and flew to Las Vegas, the grand gambling Mecca in the Nevada Desert, where he won $27,000 playing blackjack – sufficient to keep the company afloat long enough to recapitalize. It was an unorthodox and probably inadvisable strategy, but Smith considered he had more to lose by not chancing it. Without the funds to pay for the fuel to fly the planes that deliver the parcels, he reasoned, FedEx would be over anyway.

Know When to Beat a Retreat

'Quitting is not giving up, it's choosing to focus
your attention on something more important.'

OSAYI OSAR-EMOKPAE,

IMPOSSIBLE IS STUPID (2011)

According to *Forbes*, Walt Disney once said: 'The difference in winning and losing is most often not quitting.' As the previous chapter shows, there is much to be said for keeping on keeping on. However, it is also the case that sometimes the best and most responsible decision is to step away from a business. Considering that some 90 per cent of start-ups don't last the distance, this is a quandary that most entrepreneurs face at one time or another and they should not be ashamed to confront it.

In her book quoted on the previous page, Osar-Emokpae continued:'Quitting is not losing confidence, it's realizing that there are more valuable ways you can spend your time. Quitting is not making excuses, it's learning to be more productive, efficient and effective instead.' Knowing when your business is past the point of ever being a success is an essential if difficult-to-master skill for any entrepreneur.

Turning your back on an enterprise that you once thought was brilliant and destined for success is, of course, hard. But often the decision to act like an ostrich, stick your head in the ground and pretend things will be OK in the end brings greater pain. Lashing yourself to a failing business because you have a misplaced sense of determination – or because you cannot contemplate an alternative – is folly. Such a business will drain not only your financial resources but also your emotional and intellectual reserves. Far better sometimes to admit defeat, learn your lessons and prepare yourself for the next challenge. But take heart from Warren Buffett's thoughts on the subject from his 1997 collection, *The Essays*: 'Should you find yourself in a chronically leaking boat, energy devoted to changing vessels is likely to be more productive than energy devoted to patching leaks.'

Even James Dyson, the man who never gave up on his idea for a revolutionary vacuum cleaner, has had to throw in the towel on occasions. In 2017 he announced plans to start producing a radically different type of electric car from 2020. Some 400 engineers had been working since 2015 on the project valued at £2.5 billion. But in 2019, Dyson pulled the plug. According to the *Financial Times*, he emailed staff: 'Though we have tried very hard throughout the development process, we simply can no longer see a way to make it commercially viable.' It certainly represented a blow, but how much greater would the damage have been had he continued to bankroll such a programme without a chance of financial return? You can be sure, though, that Dyson will use the experience to inform his other commercial initiatives.

Richard Branson is another who has had to bite the bullet in his time. In the 1990s, he was forced to sell Virgin Records – the business that had paved the way for all his other successes – in order to keep other interests (particularly the Virgin Atlantic airline) afloat. By Branson's own admission, he cried his eyes out despite receiving a cheque for £1 billion for the business, but he knew he had no other choice if he wanted the rest of the Virgin Group to prosper. He expanded on his thinking many years later in his book *Like a Virgin*: 'So, if things don't work out, don't hesitate: Take that escape hatch. That way, when all's said and done, you will be able to gather your team, discuss what did or did not happen, and then embark on your next venture together. Not much older, but a lot wiser.'

So, what signs should an entrepreneur look out for in order to decide whether it's time to stick, twist or call it quits? If your business is struggling to gain a foothold, consider the following:

• You might not have made your fortune, but is the business going in the right direction? Slow forward momentum might yet speed up, but if you're going backwards, what can you do to reverse the direction of travel? If the answer is 'nothing', then the decision is made for you.

- Do you have a market? This question is so basic that many entrepreneurs forget to answer it. Who is there who will pay for what you have to offer? Do you have at least a few enthusiastic consumers around whom you can build a bigger community of customers?

- Do you have what it takes to see off the opposition? You might have the better offering, but do you have the muscle to win in the marketplace?

- Do you have the cash flow? Debt is not necessarily a sign of a failing start-up, but rather an inevitable feature of a new business. But if you routinely do not have the income to cover your outgoings over the longer term, your business is probably not feasible.

- Is your heart still in it? If it's not, it's probably time to leave the field of play. Being an entrepreneur should be something you enjoy (at least, most of the time). It should not make your life unhappier than it would otherwise be.

- If your business belonged to someone else, what would you objectively tell them to do?

If you conclude that your business is in terminal decline or is unlikely ever to achieve the success you hope for (the exact description of success will inevitably change from person to person), then it really is time to reach for that escape hatch. It is much better to fail and come back stronger than to go under in the process of propping up an enterprise that ought to be left to collapse.

EDSEL IS A NO-GO

One of the most famous 'time to walk away' cases in the history of commerce was the Ford Motor Company's Edsel model, released in 1958. Ford executives were convinced the Edsel was the car of the future, the one that would secure them a large chunk of the American market, just as the Model T had done decades earlier. But the American public wasn't having it. Consumers considered the car overpriced, ugly and generally below par. Ford was forced to withdraw it in 1960, having spent somewhere between $250 million and $400 million on its development, manufacture and marketing. The alternative was simply to throw good money after bad.

Surround Yourself with the Best

'The secret of my success is that we have gone
to exceptional lengths to hire the best people in
the world.'

STEVE JOBS, IN AN INTERVIEW WITH

BRENT SCHLENDER (1995)

John Donne famously wrote: 'No man is an island entire of itself; every man / is a piece of the continent, a part of the main.' The same is resolutely true of the entrepreneur. Occasionally, a single individual may have sufficient get-up-and-go to launch a business but any enterprise of significant scale soon requires a team working in unison. Surround yourself with the right people and success is yours. Get the wrong people, and soon enough the spark at the heart of even the most promising business will dim. It is not overstating the case to say that the early hires of a start-up are often the difference between make or break.

Study the advice of any business leader of standing, and it is not long before they highlight the importance of hiring well. Along with the previous quotation from Steve Jobs, here are the words of a handful of other big-hitters that give a flavour of the near universal accord on this point:

- 'We've always had, at our core, a focus on our

people and making sure that they are empowered to make decisions [...] I've always believed that by taking care of people in my companies, the rest will take care of itself.' – Richard Branson, *Screw Business as Usual* (2011)

- 'I am convinced that nothing we do is more important than hiring and developing people. At the end of the day you bet on people, not on strategies.' – Larry Bossidy, senior executive at General Electric and CEO of AlliedSignal Corporation, interviewed in the *Harvard Business Review* (1995)
- '[…] building a good team. That's what I spend a huge amount of time on. When I'm not building products I work with teams to build products.' – Mark Zuckerberg, in conversation at the Computer History Museum (2010)
- 'The key for us, number one, has always been hiring very smart people.' – Bill Gates, in an interview at the Smithsonian Institute (1993)
- 'I'd rather interview 50 people and not hire anyone than hire the wrong person.' – Jeff Bezos, in a *Fast Company* profile (2004)

Jobs had a reputation as a hard taskmaster and fearsome boss, so it is telling how much faith he put in building great teams. By his own admission, he liked to stretch people to wring out the best from them and he sought individuals who he thought would thrive when they were in 'a little over his head'. He devoted enormous energies to recruitment, a process he found personally exacting but one in which he liked to be actively involved. The saga of Apple's 1980s Mac project is instructive. There was a time in the early 1980s when the project was meandering, being something of a secondary concern to Apple at the time (behind the now much less heralded 'Lisa' project). Jef Raskin was leading the Mac team but Jobs decided a shake-up was in order. Among the changes he had in mind was the hiring of Andy Hertzfeld, who was then working on the Apple II. Jobs interviewed Hertzfeld in the morning and offered him a job in the afternoon, which Hertzfeld was keen to accept. He could start, he explained, as soon as he had tied up a few loose ends on his current project. Jobs responded by pulling the power cord from Hertzfeld's Apple II, losing all of his unsaved work. Hertzfeld was relocated to a new desk and immediately began his work on the Mac. Sure he had the right person for the task, Jobs showed his characteristically uncompromising attitude to recruitment.

Walt Disney was another who believed that the success of the whole relies on the strength of the individuals who comprise it. According to the Walt Disney Institute, Disney said: 'You can dream, create, design and build the most wonderful place in the world […] but it requires people to make the dream a reality.'

It was a lesson he had learned through hard

experience. Early in his career, he suffered a number of setbacks. In 1922, his Laugh-O-Grams studio collapsed when a deal with a distribution company fell through. His response was to set up the Disney Brothers Cartoon Studio in Hollywood alongside his brother Roy, who had the business acumen and eye for the bottom line that Walt then lacked. With a trusted business manager thus installed, he sought to fill his studio with the finest creatives he could find. In those early years, it was Ub Iwerks who helped Walt take the animated world by storm, the pair bouncing ideas off each other as they created legendary characters like Mickey Mouse. Then, from the 1930s until the 1970s, the Disney Studio almost single-handedly defined our expectations of what animated films could be, driven by a small hand-picked team of animators who came to be known as Disney's Nine Old Men – the people who could make dreams reality.

Like Jobs, Disney could be a tough boss to work for. In 1928, just as the Mickey Mouse phenomenon was taking off, he urged Iwerks: 'Show some of your old SPEED. Work like hell BOY. It is our one BIG CHANCE to make a real killing [...] You can do it – I know you can [...] Don't tell me it can't be done. It has got to be done.' In the end, it got too much for Iwerks and the pair went their separate ways. But Iwerks was still able to recognize Disney's excellence as a team-builder. In Steve Watts's *The Magic Kingdom*

(1997), Iwerks remembered the company's infancy: 'Walt was very close to his men in those early days. He would stop by the artists' offices and chat or visit, ask about their inside interests, and maybe make a few suggestions about their animation. The men loved it, and they all responded.' Team-building, after all, is not only about recruitment but retention too. A good entrepreneur knows when to stretch their employees and when to ease off the pressure so as to avoid reaching breaking point.

So, what should an entrepreneur look for in candidates to join their business? Experience is of course a great asset. No one wants an office manager who has never sat in front of a keyboard or filled up a diary before. But in looking for experience, beware of recruiting someone who has grown stale or unwilling to adapt *because* they have accumulated so much experience. Nor should experience be considered a substitute for the potential that a less experienced candidate might have. It is a truism that experience comes only once someone has been granted their first break. Successful teams, then, commonly have a blend of youthful enthusiasm and potential alongside experience.

Warren Buffett has his own take on recruitment. 'Somebody once said that in looking for people to hire,' he says, 'you look for three qualities: integrity, intelligence, and energy. And if you don't have the first, the other two will kill you.' Integrity and finding a candidate with a good cultural fit are considered by many leading business thinkers as every bit as important (and perhaps more so) than formal qualifications or a particular body of experience. However talented an employee is, their contribution will be limited if they are not truly at home in the organization. As Elon Musk noted at the SXSW Conference in 2013: 'The biggest mistake in general that I've made […] is to put too much of a weighting on somebody's talent and not enough on their personality.' Meanwhile, Sergey Brin, co-founder of Google, warned *Fortune*'s readers in 2008 about the dangers of employing someone whose primary focus is remuneration:

This is where you want to make sure you are hiring employees because they love to work here, they love to create things, and they're not here primarily for the money. Although when they do create something valuable you want to reward them. That's when things really pay off.

Speaking on AutoBild.TV in 2014, Musk eloquently expounded on his philosophy of recruitment, providing a neat summary of why it pays an entrepreneur to recruit wisely:

The ability to attract and motivate great people is critical to the success of a company because a company is a group of people that are assembled to create a product or service. That's the purpose of a company. People sometimes forget this elementary truth. If you're able to get great people to join the company and work together toward a common goal and have a relentless sense of perfection about that goal, then you will end up with a great product. And if you have a great product, lots of people will buy it, and then the company will be successful.

MORE THAN YOUR JOB'S WORTH

The interview is a standard component of the recruitment process but one that holds all sorts of peril. Steve Jobs, perhaps predictably, put his candidates through a particular brand of trauma as he looked to sort the wheat from the chaff. In order to see how quickly a candidate could think on their feet, he asked probing questions like, 'How might you investigate a technology without revealing to anyone that you're investigating it?' Other questions had a more philosophical bent, such as, 'Why are you here?' On one occasion, he goaded a candidate after they had given what he considered a weak answer by interrupting them and muttering, 'Gobble, gobble, gobble.' They did not get the job.

Build a Brand

'As nice as it is to read articles that say the Virgin brand is one of the most powerful in the world, our corporate goal is to make it one of the most trusted.'

RICHARD BRANSON, *LIKE A VIRGIN* (2012)

A company is the legal entity through which an entrepreneur generally does business, but it is the strength of the company's brand that will determine long-term success. Jeff Bezos told the Edison Nation video series in 2011: 'Brands for companies are like reputations for people. And reputations are hard-earned and easily lost.' But if people like the personality, they are more likely to come back for return business. As Starbucks CEO Howard Schultz commented in 1998: 'If people believe they share values with a company, they will stay loyal to the brand.'

A great many companies work on the basis that price is king when it comes to consumer decision-making. Certainly, there's not much mileage in pricing yourself out of the market. However, time and again, consumer studies suggest that overall customer satisfaction is the most important factor in deciding where people spend their money. Show two boxes of washing detergent to a consumer and they'll likely go for the one they know produces good results even if it's a little more expensive.

Brand trust is also why you might well end up at a familiar fast-food joint when you first arrive in a new city, as you bank on knowing exactly what you'll get even as you might suspect there are far more exciting – but, crucially, uncertain – culinary experiences to be had just around the corner.

Your brand is your opportunity to communicate to the world what your business means. What makes your enterprise different, special, essential. Why should customers come to you in the first place and keep returning? Often businesses make the mistake of thinking that successful branding is about having a memorable name and a cool logo. These things are, of course, important but they are really the end points of a much deeper process. Branding is about understanding exactly what your company and its products or services represent. What is your business's culture? What are your long-term aims? How do they coincide with the needs of your customer base? Only when you have answered these questions should you even start to think about how best to communicate the answers.

Richard Branson is of course one of the great branders of modern times. As a teenager in the 1960s, he began his commercial life by launching a magazine filled with celebrity interviews aimed at students. Within a few years, he expanded his business interests to include first a mail-order record business and then a record label. He named his enterprise Virgin, principally because he and his fledgling staff were all effectively newcomers into the business world. It was a wily one to adopt, at once evoking innocence, humour and a little bit of edginess.

Within a decade, the record label was huge off the back of signing the likes of Mike Oldfield, The Rolling Stones and The Sex Pistols. Subsequently, Branson entered entirely new business sectors, encompassing everything from an airline and hotels to radio stations, a soft-drinks company and space tourism. Today, he employs tens of thousands of people in dozens of countries. But the Virgin brand has remained a constant. In his 2008 book, *Business Stripped Bare*, his clear sense of what his brand means was obvious, 'The Virgin brand,' he said, 'is a guarantee that you'll be treated well, that you'll get a high-quality product which won't dent your bank balance, and you'll get more fun out of your purchase than you expected – whatever it is [...] No other brand has become a "way-of-life" brand the way Virgin has.'

The Virgin brand is also an object lesson in how the truly great brands manage to combine a sense of constancy – of underlying values that do not change – with the ability to evolve and adjust to changing conditions and circumstances. Even as the Virgin brand approaches its half-century, it manages to retain a sense of modernity and edginess to go alongside the values Branson cited above. Another example might be McDonald's, whose famous golden arches represent the promise of a predictable, reliable consumer experience even as the company adjusts to the challenges of providing a menu fit for a twenty-first-century diner. Scott Bedbury, an advertising and marketing guru who has worked for both Nike and Starbucks, has noted (as quoted in Idris Mootee's 2013 book, *60-Minute Brand Strategist: The Essential Brand Book for Marketing Professionals*): 'A great brand is a story that's never completely told. A brand is a metaphorical story that connects with something very deep – a fundamental appreciation of mythology. Stories create the emotional context people need to locate themselves in a larger experience.'

When you are clear on the identity and values you wish to express, it is then time to figure out how to encapsulate them in a memorable way. This is where you can agonise – possibly in the company of some branding experts – on a name and logo that sums up your enterprise. Do you want your name and visuals to be sharp and precise to reflect your 'down to business' offering (think Visa or Microsoft), or perhaps you want something stylish and aspirational (like Nike and its famous Swoosh) or something homely and welcoming (like KFC's avuncular Colonel Sanders)? As for names, it's always worth checking that they are reasonably easy to pronounce (it's not easy to maintain a brand if everybody is saying it differently) and that it can translate internationally. Rolls-Royce was once caught out when its 'Silver Mist' model name translated into a German obscenity!

Finally, send your brand out into the world to communicate your message. Sometimes the entrepreneur themselves becomes a vital part of the brand, as in the case of Branson. He has artfully used his celebrity to bolster the Virgin name for decades. For instance, his high-profile attempts to break assorted hot-air ballooning records in the 1980s and 1990s proved a fantastic way to grow the idea that Virgin, like Branson, was a brand that came out of a non-standard mould, ambitious and willing to take risks. 'A good PR story,' Branson wrote in *Business Stripped Bare*, 'is infinitely more effective than a full-page ad, and a damn sight cheaper.' Similarly, consider how Jay-Z and Beyoncé use their celebrity to act as the most powerful of brand ambassadors for their own business ventures. Jay-Z once even exclaimed: 'I'm not a businessman, I'm a business, man!'

Modern businesses must also learn to use the many media platforms available to them to communicate their brand. Magazine covers, billboards and radio ads still all have their place, but so do Insta posts and YouTube videos. Because of the accessibility of social media (and the ability to post almost instantaneously), entrepreneurs must be aware more than ever that branding is a constant exercise. A rude employee or an off-the-cuff, off-message comment can cause irreparable damage to a brand in a heartbeat. So, be sure to be in control of your brand all of the time. Branson, again, was instructive on this point in a post on his 'Richard's Blog' on 7 October 2008: '[…] brands always mean something. If you don't define what the brand means, a competitor will. Apple's adverts contrasting a fit, happy, creative Mac with a fat, glum, nerdy PC tells you all you need to know about how that works. Even in the absence of competition, a betrayed brand can wreak a terrible revenge on a careless company. How many brands do you know mean "shoddy", "late", and "a rip-off"?'

Sell the Dream

'It isn't the whiskey they choose, it's the image.'

DAVID OGILVY, *OGILVY ON ADVERTISING* (1983)

For some businesses, successful branding is all about positioning your product or service as the best on the market. A washing detergent, for instance, wants a brand that people associate with the best cleaning results – the whitest whites and the brightest colours. Any business that creates a brand recognized as elite in its field is doing pretty well. In many cases, there is no need to do anything more. That said, we live in a world of super-brands, many of which are less about extolling the specific virtues of a good or service than they are about establishing a link in the consumer's mind between that brand and a whole way of life. Such brands are selling not so much a product as a dream of how good your life can be if you give them your custom.

This is the point that British advertising guru David Ogilvy was making on the previous page. 'Take whiskey,' he wrote. 'Why do some people choose Jack Daniel's, while others choose Grand Dad or Taylor? Have they tried all three and compared the taste?

Don't make me laugh. The reality is that these three brands have different images which appeal to different kinds of people. It isn't the whiskey they choose, it's the image. The brand image is 90 per cent of what the distiller has to sell.' He went as far as to suggest that you could give a consumer a taste of Old Crow (telling them it was such) and then give them another taste (but this time telling them it's Jack Daniel's). They will think the two drinks are quite different, he argued: 'They are tasting images.'

Often, advertising slogans provide a good indicator as to whether a brand is 'product focused' or something more aspirational. Domestos bleach, for instance, used the slogan 'Kills all known germs. Dead.' This told consumers all they needed to know about the effectiveness of the product. Use Domestos, the campaign suggested, and you'll have a really clean toilet. That was what people wanted of the product – not that Domestos would make them feel super-cool, extra popular, unburdened of all worries or generally improved as a person in some other respect.

Yet other products are all about communicating that somehow you will feel different and better for using their wares. Consider, say, a super-brand like Coca-Cola. Its slogans over the years have included: 'Taste the feeling', 'Catch the wave' and 'It's the Real Thing'. None of these actually tell anything about the drink itself, in terms of its tastes or potential physiological benefits. Instead, they arouse an emotional response. The first suggests that Coke will give the drinker 'that feeling' they long for, the second conjures up images of surfing on sun-drenched seas, and the third that the drink somehow has a stamp of authenticity. Nike, meanwhile, has long urged its customer base to 'Just do it' in another campaign that offers little insight into the specific qualities of the product but instead leaves its audience wondering whether wearing a pair of Nikes might help them achieve their unfulfilled goals. Then there is the case of Marlboro, whose advertising sidestepped the thorny issue of whether smoking can ever be good for you to suggest that by buying the product you could 'Come to Marlboro Country', where every man could live the dream of being a John Wayne-esque cowboy.

Richard Branson has claimed that 'no other brand has become a "way of life" brand the way Virgin has', yet arguably the king of the dream-sellers in recent times was Steve Jobs. While Jobs was at the helm of Apple, its customers sometimes seemed more like brand disciples than run-of-the-mill consumers. At a time when Apple seemed pitched in an arm-wrestle with Microsoft for dominance of the personal-computer business, people tended to be on one team or the other. Apple's supporters might follow their team's fortunes with the same sort of passion usually reserved for sports fans. Product launches, at which

Jobs gave a glimpse of the latest wonders to be added to the Apple roster, became global media events. Jobs, in his trademark black roll-neck and with a bewitching presentational style, left his audience feeling like they were being given a glimpse of the future – a future they could be a part of. He was a master at his work, selling not merely the latest high-tech gadgetry but the very aspiration to a lifestyle.

In 1984, Apple ran a landmark advert in the middle of the Super Bowl. This in itself was a grand statement of intent. The company was signalling that its computers were for a mass market like never before; computers were no longer the preserve of corporations or technology geeks but were for the sort of average Joes who watched the Super Bowl. The advert itself became an instant classic. It was a short film, directed by Hollywood heavyweight Ridley Scott (whose back catalogue included the legendary *Blade Runner*) and based on George Orwell's dystopian masterpiece, *1984*. An Everywoman heroine was filmed running through an Orwellian landscape, carrying a stylized picture of a Macintosh computer before smashing a representation of Big Brother. 'You'll see why 1984 won't be like "1984",' ran the slogan. The subtext was multilayered but clear: Apple customers are natural rebels, freedom fighters, seekers of a better future – and definitely not like the company's 'Big Brother-esque' rivals. Buy an Apple, the advert suggested, and you are not buying a computer so much as asserting your attitude to life and the world around you.

It was a hugely effective selling strategy and one that Jobs championed throughout his career. The iconic iPod campaign, for example, featured silhouetted figures enjoying their music collections through discreet earbuds. There was little in the way of detailed product specification but the message got through: buy this product and escape into your own world of music. Apple's branding was minimal for that campaign but everyone knew whose product it was. And still today, Apple campaigns tend to focus less on product detail and more on how the product will make you feel. Selling the dream.

David Ogilvy once observed: 'You cannot bore people into buying your product; you can only interest them in buying it.' If you can persuade an audience not only that your product does what it's meant to, but also that their lives will be significantly better as a result, you will have gone a long way to snaring their interest. It is up to each individual entrepreneur to determine the right course for their particular business. Everyone wants a clean loo, but few people spend their lives dreaming about it. If your business can convincingly promise to take them a little closer to what does fill their dreams, though, your bottom line is likely to see the benefits too.

DARING TO THINK DIFFERENTLY

Steve Jobs oversaw arguably the greatest of all Apple's advertising campaigns: the 'Think Different' campaign that ran from 1997 to 2002. It served as a virtual manifesto for the company, celebrating 'the crazy ones. The misfits, the rebels, the troublemakers [...] The ones who see things differently.' The campaign used the images of such icons as Mahatma Gandhi, Albert Einstein, Pablo Picasso and Martin Luther King – people who had never themselves used an Apple Product but (so it was being suggested) surely would have done given the chance. The campaign celebrated all those 'crazy enough' to think they can change the world. It was the perfect harmony of commercial branding and elevated aspiration and cemented Jobs's reputation as the best in the dream-selling business.

Don't be Afraid to Disrupt

'To the disrupters go the spoils.'

HEATHER SIMMONS, *REINVENTING DELL:*

THE INNOVATION IMPERATIVE (2015)

The phrase 'disruptive innovation' was coined by academic and business consultant Clayton M. Christensen in his 1995 essay 'Disruptive Technologies: Catching the Wave' (co-written with Joseph Bower). But what does it mean to be a business disruptor? In short, it means to shake up the status quo. A disruptor is an entrepreneur who comes up with a new product or service, or maybe even just a new way of doing old things, whose ideas eventually come to displace those of the established players in a market. As Heather Simmons noted: 'Those who disrupt their industries change consumer behaviour, alter economics, and transform lives.'

Disruptors can – and do – exist in all sectors but many of the most famous entrepreneurial disruptors of the twenty-first century come from the technology industry. Think of how Bill Gates changed the face of computing, how Mark Zuckerberg altered how we connect with other people, how Jeff Bezos made us change the way we have shopped for centuries, or how

Steve Jobs changed our approach to listening to music or using a phone. There is no doubt that we live in a Golden Age of disruption. Such disruption is obviously bad for those companies that are unable to respond, but where one business withers, another can prosper – and all to the benefit of the consumer, who naturally gains from the improvements brought by the incoming disruptor. As Elon Musk noted in PandoMonthly in 2012: 'In certain sectors, like automotive and solar and space, you don't see new entrants […] but it's really new entrants that drive innovation more than anything.'

Yet even as the individuals listed above were at the heart of various commercial whirlwinds, the disruptor-entrepreneur does well to remember that change generally comes slowly. What might to the consumer seem like a blink-of-an-eye development customarily results from a period of years of innovation. The uber-success of, for example, Microsoft and Apple from the 1980s was built on the back of years of hard work and experience gained by their figureheads. Amazon, meanwhile, might have changed the culture of retail but continues to face competition from traditional retailing models some quarter of a century after it was founded. Even Facebook has still not quite seen off the competition posed by the telephone and the email (and even snail-mail has not died off altogether, as some expected it to). So, if you want to make it as a disruptor, you'll need resilience and a lot of patience.

Don't be Afraid to Disrupt

Although Clayton M. Christensen gave life to the concept, the roots of disruptive innovation can be traced further back. In particular, it shares much in common with the ideas put forward earlier in the twentieth century by the Austrian economist Joseph Schumpeter. In his 1942 magnum opus, *Capitalism, Socialism and Democracy*, he wrote about the 'gale of creative destruction' as the 'process of industrial mutation that incessantly revolutionizes the economic structure from within, incessantly destroying the old one, incessantly creating a new one'. That is to say, economies (and societies) progress by coming up with new ideas that replace the old ways of doing things. Schumpeter in turn sourced his ideas in part from Karl Marx, who regarded all of human history as a process of one economic model overturning another. (Marx, of course, believed that capitalism was destined to give way to communism, which today seems less likely than ever.)

If the internet revolution is the latest iteration of large-scale disruptive innovation (or, alternatively, creative destruction), it in some ways resembles the Industrial Revolution of the eighteenth and nineteenth centuries. Indeed, the Industrial Revolution was in many respects even more dramatic, marking a decisive move away from local, small-scale businesses to large-scale industry that sought to serve not merely local villages or towns but whole countries and continents at a time. It ushered in the age of globalization (for better and worse) and in many countries saw the relocation of entire communities away from rural to urban settings. Many historians still regard the Industrial Revolution as the birth of the modern world. All of which is to say that economic success and entrepreneurial disruption have long gone together.

Of course, not every entrepreneur is interested in destroying the old systems and creating new ones. Many are content with simply gaining a foothold in an existing market. Yet even then it is essential to look at what that market's existing players are doing and seek to do it better and differently. Some disruption is profound – think of the Amazon retail model or Henry Ford's moving construction line. But other disruption can be much subtler, its impact far more incremental. As Jay Samit, a digital-media innovator and author of *Disrupt You! Master Personal Transformation, Seize Opportunity, and Thrive in the Era of Endless Innovation* (2015), has written: 'Disruptors don't have to discover something new; they just have to discover a practical use for new discoveries.' Without any disruption, the consumer will have no reason to switch to a new enterprise from a business they already know.

All entrepreneurism must then carry at least a seed of disruptiveness: a business is pointless unless it aims to enter and disrupt an existing market (or, much more rarely, create an entirely new market). Fortunately, though, the 'new kid on the block' entrepreneur has a greater capacity for disruption than those already in situ, which gives them a significant advantage. As Christensen put it: 'The reason why it is so difficult for existing firms to capitalize on disruptive innovations is that their processes and their business model that make them good at the existing business actually make them bad at competing for the disruption.'

In the 1870s, Christopher Sholes created a commercial disruption that did not immediately send the world into a spiral but was nonetheless profound and long-lasting. Wanting to improve upon existing typewriters, he came up with the QWERTY keyboard we still use today – specially designed to overcome the then prevalent problem of clashing keys when commonly used letters were too close together. Sholes himself suspected his act of disruption would 'have its brief day and be thrown aside'. But disruption does not necessarily need to be seismic to be profound.

And of course, for some entrepreneurs, seismic disruption is the absolute goal. A Jobs or a Musk never entered into a market content to make a few ripples. For them, major disruption is the whole point. In Musk's own words to the 2013 SXSW Conference: 'I do think it's worth thinking about whether what you're doing is going to result in disruptive change or not. If it's just incremental, it's unlikely to be something major. It's got to be substantially better than what's gone on before.'

HITTING THE RIGHT NOTES

The music industry was at the centre of one of the most striking episodes of destructive / disruptive innovation of recent times. At its heart was a new technology: file-sharing via the internet. Such sharing was initially illegal but when it became impossible to police (and so save a huge drop-off in the sale of physical music formats like CDs and vinyl), the industry adapted and worked with legal file-sharing entities like iTunes and Spotify. Today, over half of industry revenues come from downloads and streaming.

Scale Up

'For me, the most fun is change or growth [...]
Launching a business is kind of like a motorboat:
you can go very quickly and turn fast.'

TONY HSIEH, CEO OF ZAPPOS.COM, 2009

As we have seen, no business emerges fully formed. All of them start with a first customer or client. Every successful enterprise must by definition go through a period of growth. It is how an entrepreneur prepares their business for scaling up that marks out the runaway successes from the could-have-beens.

That is not to say that the success of a business can be judged only by its scale. Some entrepreneurs prefer to stay relatively small, content perhaps that over-expansion will damage their ability to service their clients' needs to a sufficient standard or that their business model caters for a local need and is unsuited to widespread replication.

But even these types of entrepreneur will want to drive their business forward, increasing inputs to expand output and maximize profitability. And those who want to be commercial giants need to think in terms of expanding their business from a local enterprise to become a national concern and then, ultimately, a player on the international stage. To do so

successfully, here are four fundamental factors to keep
in mind:

- If you want to become big, you need to think big.
  If you're content for your business to tick over,
  that's fine. But if you want it to be a world-beater,
  you need a world-beater's mindset. As James Cash
  Penney, founder of the J. C. Penney department
  store, has noted: 'Growth is never by mere chance; it
  is the result of forces working together.'
- Don't forget what makes your business scalable in
  the first place. Roy Kroc, who built the McDonald's
  empire, realized the importance of keeping up
  the standards that originally made customers love
  the company's product. 'We provide food that
  customers love, day after day after day,' he said.
  'People just want more of it.'
- Prepare your company for growing pains.
  Expansion brings inevitable problems but an
  entrepreneur should do everything possible to ready
  their business. Make sure, for instance, that your IT
  systems are robust enough to meet higher demand,
  that your team of employees is large enough, that
  your supply chain is in place and that you have
  sufficient cash flow to deal with a few inevitable
  hiccups. The tale of the demise of US health-
  technology company Theranos is complex and
  already legendary. But one root cause of its failure

was a desire to expand before it had the very basics
– a working, scalable blood-testing system of the
type it had promised to the market – ready to roll
out. In other words, it got way ahead of itself.

- Try to predict what lies ahead. This is no easy
matter, especially in the worlds of finance and
business. Forecasting is a famously inexact science;
that said, if you don't base your plans on solid
analysis of what is likely to happen in the short
to mid-term as a bare minimum, then failure is
almost inevitable. At the very least, going through
the process will help you focus on obstacles that
you will likely face. Don't do what the owners
of Crumbs Bake Shop did after they bought the
business (which had launched in 2003) for $66
million in 2011. Within three years its share price
had plummeted from $13 to $0.15. Its downfall:
the failure to spot that the seemingly exponential
growth in the popularity of cupcakes (then its
complete product offering) would ever come to
an end.

The example of Ray Kroc and McDonald's is instructive
to any aspiring entrepreneur, as it ranks among the
greatest scalings-up of all time. Moreover, it was not
even Kroc's own business. The original McDonald's
restaurant was a no-frills, self-service takeaway burger
bar in San Bernardino, California, run by two brothers,

Dick and Mac McDonald. Its menu was simple – burgers, fries and milkshakes – and everything was quickly delivered to customers by production line. Ray Kroc, a fifty-something travelling milkshake-mixer salesman, was deeply impressed when he dropped in one day and surveyed the happy faces that filled the joint.

He also figured that the business was turning over a lot of money. Then he began to imagine the riches to be had by expanding the business into a chain, each branch replicating the qualities of this original restaurant. Emboldened, he met with the McDonald brothers and asked if they might be interested in going into partnership with him. They were not. They were happy with the business as it was and had no great desire to take on the extra work of expansion.

He was not to be deterred, though. If they did not have the necessary mindset, he certainly did. He negotiated a deal with them that allowed him to license the name and replicate their catering model. He then set about selling franchises. But whereas some franchise businesses are happy to take a franchisee's money and then leave them to it, Kroc recognized that long-term success relied on scaling up the San Bernardino model with all its attributes.

Consistency was the key. Customers needed to know that they could expect the same standard of food and quality of service regardless of which McDonald's they were in. In order to ensure that every restaurant used the same quality ingredients and the identical processes to turn them into burgers, fries and milkshakes, Kroc envisaged a franchise model based on a three-legged stool. The central McDonald's organization was one leg, the franchisee was the second and the suppliers the third. As he liked to tell prospective investors: 'In business for yourself, but not by yourself.'

He demanded unstinting discipline as the business scaled up. The composition of burgers was codified in a seventy-five-page manual detailing the 'McDonald's Method'. Standards of service were to be undeviating too. As he noted in his memoir, *Grinding It Out*: 'McDonald's is a people business, and that smile on that counter girl's face when she takes your order is a vital part of our image.'

Within three years of the Kroc-inspired scaling-up, McDonald's had sold its hundred-millionth burger. By 1963, that figure had reached a billion and in 1974 the business was valued at more than the entire US steel industry. Kroc was proud that his company took 'the hamburger business more seriously than anyone else'. He was also never content to let the business stand still. 'As long as you're green, you're growing,' he said. 'As soon as you're ripe, you start to rot.'

In more recent times, Zuckerberg has taken Facebook on a comparable trajectory. From the humble social-networking service serving students at Harvard, through gradual growth that took in first other Ivy League Colleges and then universities and high schools across the country, he built the company into the global behemoth that it is today, with well over 2 billion active users.

Of course, it has not all been plain sailing; but whatever criticisms the social-media platform might attract, there is no doubting Zuckerberg's brilliance in understanding his market and preparing his company to meet its demands. Certainly not everything he and Facebook have done has worked, but whenever something has gone commercially wrong, Facebook has been robust enough to deal with it – even as so many social-media competitors have come and gone. Moreover, it has rarely lost sight that its growth relies on continuing to provide what the market demands.

For all Zuckerberg's sporadic swashbuckling outbursts, he is a man who has guided Facebook's scaling-up through vision combined with attention to detail. Silicon Valley 'is a little short-term focused and that bothers me', he said in a 2011 interview at Y Combinator's Startup School in Palo Alto, California. Keeping his business fit for purpose for the long term on an ever-expanding stage has seemingly been his principal motivation. As he told ABC's Diane Sawyer in 2010: 'People don't care about what someone says about you in a movie – or even what you say, right? They care about what you build.'

Streamline

'To make an ever-increasingly large quantity of goods of the best possible quality, to make them in the best and most economical fashion, and to force them out onto the market.'

HENRY FORD ON 'BUSINESS FUNDAMENTALS'

(1930)

Many entrepreneurs start their businesses as cottage industries, where they are responsible for many if not all aspects of the running. They will be the brains behind the operation, coming up with the initial idea, tailoring the good or service being offered, overseeing admin, networking, building the brand, making the tea and much more besides.

But the chances are that the more successful a business becomes, the less suitable it is to be run in this sort of way. Expansion tends to go hand in hand with the need for increased efficiency. In certain ways, a small start-up has advantages in efficiency that larger, more established organizations will always struggle to compete with. As we will see elsewhere in this book, for instance, a start-up can by its nature move faster and respond more flexibly to changing market conditions than a large corporation.

Nonetheless, a bigger business has its natural advantages too. Big businesses can, for example, exploit economies of scale. Often, having the capacity to produce more makes it possible to produce each unit at a lower cost. Imagine you have two bakeries next to each other. They have identical premises but Baker A has the capital to install only one oven while Baker B could afford two ovens. They each have an assistant and Baker A's staff together spend five hours per day producing 200 loaves from their one oven. However, Baker B's staff can produce 400 loaves in six hours. (It doesn't take them much more effort to make the extra dough to fill both their ovens.) As a result, Baker B is spending less money per loaf than Baker A, since the extra he spends on ingredients, energy costs and labour costs is quickly absorbed by the extra revenue he generates from having twice as much stock to sell. Baker B is more successful because his business is the more streamlined in terms of production.

There are many ways to make sure your business stays streamlined even as it grows. You could, for instance:

- Establish a 'best practice' guide that is regularly reviewed. This way you can ensure that your employees are working to the same standards as you yourself adhere to.
- Review emerging technologies to see if they may be able to help you improve the efficiency of your business.
- Impose an effective training regime so that staff are constantly renewing and updating their knowledge.
- Even when business is good, always look for the fat

that can be trimmed and for anything that might in due course serve as a block on the smooth operation of your business.

- Get an outsider's view. No one knows your business like you but a mentor or an independent third party might be able to spot potential spanners in the works to which you have become blind.

Often, technological advances are key to streamlining. The telephone and the typewriter were two inventions that utterly changed the way that successful organizations did business. More recently, the internet revolution has allowed many astute entrepreneurs to streamline their business ideas so that they are fit for the modern consumer. Jeff Bezos, for instance, took the traditional retail model and re-sculpted it for the e-commerce age – and in the process made himself one of the world's richest men. Yet we must go a little further back into history to find the man who perhaps did more to streamline industrial production than anyone else in history: Henry Ford.

Ford's entrepreneurial dream was outrageously simple and brilliant. While car ownership had been a luxury that only the very wealthiest in society could enjoy, Ford dreamed of mass-producing cars cheaply enough that ordinary working people could buy them. He achieved this aim with the launch of his Model T car, a vehicle that for decades ranked as the world's bestselling car. But in order to get it to market, Ford had to come up with a whole new way of manufacturing.

The Model T came out in 1908 priced at $825. It was much cheaper than its major commercial rivals but still very expensive for the average man or woman in the street. Sales started well enough but Ford realized that to achieve the sales he aspired to he needed to knock a chunk off the price. He was unwilling to compromise on engineering quality but kept other design features simple and down-to-earth. He understood that his buyers did not expect the luxury synonymous with, say, Rolls-Royce – hence his famous observation: 'Any customer can have a car painted any colour that he wants so long as it's black.' (Black paint was the quickest-drying and cheapest finish available at the time.)

Before Ford, the assembly line was used for fairly simple production processes, such as might be found in mills, breweries and bakeries. But Ford was the first to use it in something as complex as car manufacture. Until then, a team of engineers worked on a single car, but Ford had the vision to turn the process about-face. The car, he decreed, would move from one specialist worker to another, each carrying out a discrete part of the manufacturing process. Over a period of five years, he perfected a system in which each car went through eighty-four distinct processes. He also built a bespoke power-driven assembly line so that it was no longer necessary for vehicles to be moved about by a cumbersome system of ropes and pulleys. Introduced in 1913, his new system reduced the construction time of a car from about twelve hours to two and a half. Within a year, Model Ts accounted for half the cars sold in the USA. As of 1922, the price tag of each vehicle had fallen to less than $300.

Justus George Frederick's 1930 work *A Philosophy of Production: A Symposium*, gives us an insight into Ford's thinking. 'Through all the years that I have been in business,' Ford said, 'I have never yet found our business bad as a result of any outside force. It has always been due to some defect in our own company, and whenever we located and repaired that defect our business became good again – regardless of what anyone else might be doing.' He then laid out what he considered to be the 'fundamental principles of business', which included those listed in the quotation at the beginning of this chapter. 'These fundamentals are all summed up in the single word "service",' he said. 'The service starts with discovering what people need and then supplying that need according to the principles that have just been given.'

One hundred years on, Elon Musk has followed Ford into the realm of motor manufacturing and echoes his philosophy on always striving for efficiency: 'Constantly think,' Musk has said, 'about how you can do things better and question yourself.'

Grow into Yourself Graciously

'Google, an enormously successful company, claims a sweeping right to appropriate the property of others for its own commercial use, unless it is told, case by case and instance by instance, not to.'

STATEMENT BY ASSOCIATION OF AMERICAN UNIVERSITY PRESSES (2005)

The previous statement was made in response to Google's mammoth book-digitizing project. The scheme began in 2002, with the ultimate aim of digitally scanning most of the world's books to create a vast online library. To its advocates, it was one of the greatest humanistic projects ever undertaken. To many writers and publishers, however, who were fearful that they would no longer be able to earn revenue from their books, it posed an existential threat. The project eventually became bogged down in lengthy and costly legal disputes – though not before some 25 million books were scanned.

An awe-inspiring attempt to harness a vast resource of learning and cultural importance, or a gross corporate abuse of long-established copyright law? Opinion remains as divided today as it ever was. Whatever your own feelings, such episodes highlight a serious quandary for the aspiring entrepreneur. The more successful you get, the less of the swashbuckling outsider you become. Whereas you were once perceived as the plucky underdog, shaking things up for the general good, your actions may quickly start to be reinterpreted as those of a commercial bully. It is a line that can be immensely difficult to walk.

Google's motto used to be 'Don't be evil' and this remains part of its corporate code of conduct today. Yet Google has repeatedly found itself under attack as it has struggled to transition from innovative disruptor to established market behemoth. Over the years, Google and several other Silicon Valley giants have variously been accused of breaching antitrust legislation and copyright law, practising forms of censorship in politically sensitive regions of the world, misappropriating and misusing customer data, abusing labour conventions and avoiding tax.

The problems these companies face in transitioning from the role of outsider-disruptor is encapsulated by an editorial that appeared in the *Observer* newspaper (17 March 2018) after revelations about Facebook's role in the Cambridge Analytica scandal (see box at end of chapter). 'Shortly after Facebook became a public company,' the editorial read, 'its founder famously exhorted his employees to "move fast and break things". It was, of course, a hacker's trope and, as such, touchingly innocent. What perhaps never occurred to Zuckerberg is that liberal democracy might be one of the things they break. It's time for him – and them – to grow up.' The truly successful entrepreneur must somehow navigate that path from youthful prodigy to responsible maturity. All without losing the energy and fizz that drove the enterprise in the first place.

It is a challenge particularly acute in businesses whose reach stretches across the globe and whose customer base might comprise billions of people. But if it is any consolation, this is by no means a new problem. Take the case of John D. Rockefeller, for example. Having set up the Standard Oil Company in 1870, he came to dominate the American oil industry. It is estimated that at his peak, he controlled 90 per cent of all US oil and amassed a fortune equivalent to 2 per cent of US GDP. In building his business, Rockefeller took advantage of technical innovations and corporate structuring but he was also known for his ruthlessness in eliminating commercial rivals by means that were at times, to put it kindly, on the very edge of legitimacy. Finally, in 1911, the Supreme Court ruled that he had contravened antitrust laws and that Standard Oil should thus be split up. Rockefeller was unable to avoid his own transformation from the disruptor to the obstructive behemoth, and so the authorities were forced to intervene and free up the market once more. His is certainly a cautionary tale for the modern generation of disruptors. As Friedrich Nietzsche observed in *Beyond Good and Evil* (1886): 'Whoever fights monsters should see to it that in the process he does not become a monster.'

DATA WITH DESTINY

In 2018 Facebook found itself the focal point of a media storm as it was revealed that Cambridge Analytica, a political consulting firm, had been able to harvest the personal data of tens of millions of Facebook users, which Cambridge Analytica then used to direct political advertising campaigns. Although Facebook did not provide the data directly, the episode exposed frailties in the governance of personal data. In the immediate aftermath, Facebook suffered a $100 billion-plus decrease on its market capitalization value. Moreover, Mark Zuckerberg was summoned to give evidence in front of the US Congress.

Remodel the Landscape

'I spend my life building the world
I want to live in…'

ROBIN CHASE, FOUNDER OF ZIPCAR,
QUOTED IN THE *GUARDIAN* (2013)

As the previous chapter showed, dreams come in all different forms. One entrepreneur might dream of having the most popular restaurant in the neighbourhood, another to create the make-up range used by the stars and bought by their millions of fans, and a third to build a city in outer space.

All have equal validity. Sometimes it is true, too, that the entrepreneur with the seemingly more humble aspirations ends up happiest. It may well be that the neighbourhood restaurateur has a life every bit as joyous (and maybe even more so) than the household name who runs a business empire that earns them billions. There is room in the world for both the entrepreneur who wants to do something well and make a good living from it and their counterpart who wants to change the very fabric of society. This chapter, though, is particularly interested in the latter.

Robin Chase co-founded the car-sharing business Zipcar in 2000 and may be counted among those contributing to the alteration of the global commercial landscape. She was one of the first to bring the concept of car sharing to the USA, having seen several successful car-sharing enterprises in Europe. It is an idea that has changed the way millions of people think about how they travel and which has had significant environmental benefits too, in reducing the overall number of cars on the road. Expanding to the *Guardian* on her claim of 'building the world I want to live in', Chase spoke of developing a society of 'high integrity, where we care about sources and consequences of our lifestyle, where individuals and companies thrive in a mutually beneficial and delightfully efficient system, where opportunities to participate and engage abound'. Zipcar, then, stands at the frontier between commerce and a deeper social evolution.

Sometimes game-changing ideas are not easy to spot. In 1854, vast crowds gathered at the Crystal Palace at New York's World's Fair to watch a demonstration by one Elisha Otis. He stood on a platform that hung four storeys high, held only by a solitary rope connected to a wooden frame. After a while, the rope was dramatically severed with a sword, yet Otis did not plummet to his death. Instead, his patented safety brake clicked into action. Word soon got around about Otis's 'safety elevator' and orders rushed in to have the system fitted into multistorey buildings to transport goods and people between floors. (It had been the legendary showman P.T. Barnum's idea to turn what was essentially a product launch into a perilous crowd-pleasing 'event'.) Within a few years, Otis's invention made it possible to build ever-higher buildings, paving the way for the urban skyscapes that dominate cities across the planet today. But who in those New York audiences realized the implication as they stood in awe while Otis declared, 'All safe, gentlemen, all safe.'

In recent decades, Silicon Valley has been home to perhaps more 'landscape changers' than anywhere else in the world. Gates, Jobs, Zuckerberg, Larry Page and Sergey Brin… the list goes on of those who have harnessed technology to radically redefine how swathes of the world behave and even think about themselves. Another among them is Arianna Huffington, who has had a pivotal role in the changing nature of media consumption since setting up the *Huffington Post* in 2005. At a time when most of the world received its news via professional journalists operating through traditional media outlets, Huffington saw the potential for a new type of news site. The *Huffington Post* started life as part news-amalgamator (pointing users towards syndicated news stories from multiple sources) and part blog. It encouraged commentary pieces from a range of voices (and not necessarily from established journalists) and included subject matter ranging from serious politics to entertainment, health, technology, culture and much more besides.

Not everyone was convinced by the formula but

Huffington realized that the new generation of tech-savvy consumers wanted the ability to curate their news consumption, rather than being fed a selected tranche by traditional newspapers or television bulletins. Key to Huffington's success was her determination not to be blown off course by the non-believers. As she has said: 'The more we refuse to buy into our inner critics – and our external ones too – the easier it will get to have confidence in our choices and to feel comfortable with who we are.'

Such was the website's success that it was bought by AOL for over $300 million in 2011. By then, Huffington's name was a regular entrant in the 'most influential' lists of magazines like *Time* and *Forbes*. Certainly, she was instrumental in setting out a blueprint for the new age of media consumption. Many followed where she first trod, not least among them Breitbart. com. With the *Huffington Post* (now called *HuffPost*) widely acknowledged as a bastion of liberal values, it was perhaps ironic that it was Andrew Breitbart, one of Huffington's trusted lieutenants, who set up the eponymous website known for its right-leaning tendencies and its championing of Donald Trump for the presidency.

But such ironies are part and parcel of the difficult and complex process of changing the world. Altering the commercial and cultural landscape is always likely to throw up unforeseen consequences, and not always good ones. As he developed Facebook, for instance, Mark Zuckerberg surely could not have foretold that his bid to 'connect the world' would render his company open to accusations that it has assisted dissemination of falsehoods and undesirable content around the globe. Nor was Karl Benz able to stare into a crystal ball to see how his patent for the automobile might play its role in heating up the planet to dangerously high levels a century and a bit later. Equally, for all the now apparent downsides of social media and the combustion engine, who can today envisage a world where they did not exist? Attempting to calculate the full profit-to-loss ratios of having either is a fool's errand. What we do know is that both phenomena fundamentally changed the human environment.

In 2014 the American television producer and writer Shonda Rhimes gave a graduation address at Dartmouth College in New Hampshire. 'Dreams are lovely,' she said. 'But they are just dreams. Fleeting, ephemeral, pretty. But dreams do not come true just because you dream them. It's hard work that makes things happen. It's hard work that creates change.' It is a credo shared by that strata of entrepreneurs whose business ambitions merge with a desire to alter the very landscape of their societies.

WHERE CREDIT'S DUE

Frank Sullivan is another of the 'game changers', although it is unlikely that even he foresaw the far-reaching consequences of his business idea. Having once been embarrassed to find himself presented with the bill in a restaurant only to discover he had forgotten his wallet, he came up with the idea of the Diners Club card to avoid a repeat incident. This was the forerunner to the credit card, which made it possible for consumers to borrow money more easily than ever before. Sullivan altered not only the mechanics of making a purchase, but also the way billions of consumers think about what they can afford and when they can have it.

Play the Long Game

'Life's road is very long, but it is travelled fast.'

CARLOS SLIM, CARLOSSLIM.COM (1994)

Patience is not a characteristic that sits easily with many entrepreneurs. Entrepreneurialism tends rather to the opposite, in fact. It attracts restless spirits, eager to get on and do, often in the hope of securing their fortunes sooner rather than later. But patience is a key element in being able to take a strategic, long-term view that ultimately ensures that the really great entrepreneurs have longevity.

From his Mexican base, Carlos Slim has built a vast business empire straddling real estate, financial services, hospitality, media and entertainment, technology, energy, transport and manufacturing. For many years he has found himself ranked among the ten or so richest individuals in the world. While he could never be accused of allowing his business interests to meander, he has nonetheless spoken on numerous occasions of the dangers of getting caught up in a short-term (or, worse still, backward-looking) view of the world. As he wrote in his 'Letter to Young People' back in 1994: 'Live the present intensely and fully, do not let the past be a burden, and let the future be an incentive...'

In 1923, the economist John Maynard Keynes wrote *A Tract on Monetary Reform* in which he famously pronounced: 'In the long run we are all dead.' He was attacking economic forecasters whom he believed cited the 'long run' as a means to justify their lack of efficacy. It is, he argued 'too easy, too useless a task, if in tempestuous seasons they can only tell us, that when the storm is long past, the ocean is flat again'. It is true, too, that an entrepreneur is doomed if they use the 'long term' as cover for their failings in the short term. In other words, it is destructive to ignore what is happening today by convincing oneself that it will have all worked itself out by this time next year. Such behaviour has less to do with justified patience and long-term thinking than it does self-delusion.

But every successful business is to a lesser or greater degree a testament to patience and long-range strategy. As Jeff Bezos is recorded as saying in the Edison Nation video series of 2011: 'It's easy to have ideas. It's very hard to turn an idea into a successful product. There are many steps in between, and it takes persistence.' Warren Buffett, investor extraordinaire, also argues for playing the long game. He has spent his extraordinary career seeking investments into businesses built for long-term stability, repeatedly making the case that investors should aim to avoid selling quickly in response to short-term market fluctuations but instead look for enterprises underpinned by sound basic value, secure management and limited exposure to risk – a pretty good guide to what any business should be aspiring too.

Rovio, the Finnish company behind the mega-successful *Angry Birds* franchise, is relatively recent evidence of the power of long-term thinking. Founded in 2003 by three Helsinki University of Technology students – Niklas Hed, Jarno Väkeväinen and Kim Dikert – the company was struggling when, in 2007, the iPhone was released. Rovio realized that this was a game changer for games makers and so set about designing something that could capitalize on the app boom then taking off. On its release in 2009, *Angry Birds* was Rovio's fifty-second attempt at a suitable game. But it was by no means an immediate success. Uptake was slow in the key US and UK markets so Rovio concentrated on gaining traction in several smaller markets. Soon, it was a bestseller in countries including the Czech Republic, Denmark, Finland, Greece and Sweden. A few months later, the UK and US markets followed suit. By 2011, 75 million users were playing for 200 million minutes a day (that's sixteen years of game-time every hour) as the company raked in tens of millions of dollars on their original $100,000 investment in the game. It was an overnight success almost a decade in the making, the culmination of years of dedicated strategic planning.

Being able to find the balance between acting decisively in the day-to-day and keeping an eye on long-term strategy is a characteristic found among virtually all of the entrepreneurial greats. It is not an easy skill to master, though. The minutiae of everyday business has a habit of getting in the way, so that firefighting the latest problem often takes precedence over assessing the problem's magnitude in terms of the enterprise's long-term health. Moreover, many of us have a tendency to vastly overestimate what can be achieved in the short term (think of the impossibly long to-do lists we set ourselves) while underestimating what might be achieved in the long term. The spirit-sapping, overly long itinerary can end up serving as an obstruction, rather than an aid, to our long-term aspirations.

Of course, an entrepreneur must engage with the day-to-day, but it ought not to be at the cost of your long-term plans. Don't be tempted to go for the cheapest solution because it helps that month's budget, if the cheaper solution will have a retrograde impact on your business compared to paying a little extra for the better solution now. Do not, for example, be the entrepreneur who closes their shop for the day to repaint the old, rusting 'Shop Open' sign that hangs on the door. Especially when you could buy a new one from the signage business up the road! The money saved by putting your efforts into returning the sign to its former glories pales against the money lost by not having any customers in for the day. This is of course an imaginary scenario, but many businesses suffer from similar examples of short-termism without even realizing it.

Be especially wary of any interim money-saving decision that negatively impacts your customers' experience. They just may choose to do business elsewhere in the future. If you run a cafe and money is short, for instance, feel free to buy budget teabags for your own personal use but think very carefully about downgrading the tea you give to your customers, as it might mean they never return. Don't get lost in the woods because you can't see past the tree in front of you.

Mark Zuckerberg is a man who has boasted that it took him a mere week to build the first iteration of Facebook. But he also talks often about the sense of 'mission' he has for his company – the drive to grow it deep into the future. His words to *Fast Company* back in 2007 are worth heeding by any entrepreneur interested in more than just securing a fast buck. 'I'm here to build something for the long term,' he said. 'Anything else is a distraction.'

Negotiation is an Art

'A negotiator should observe everything. You must
be part Sherlock Holmes, part Sigmund Freud.'

VICTOR KIAM, *GOING FOR IT! HOW TO*

SUCCEED AS AN ENTREPRENEUR (1987)

Victor Kiam, quoted on the previous page, certainly knew how to get a good deal. He was the man who in 1979 bought personal-care company Remington Products in one of the first leveraged buyouts (a deal in which borrowed money is used to finance a purchase, with the assets of the company being acquired serving as collateral on the loan). Remington had for years operated in the red, but was turning a healthy profit within a year of Kiam's takeover. He became famous across the world for his claim that after his wife had bought him his first Remington electric shaver, 'I liked the shaver so much, I bought the company.'

Many of us, however, find ourselves in the same class of deal-maker as comedian Phil Wang, who once described his attempts to barter for a trinket in an Indonesian market. 'I haggled for this,' he assured his audience. 'The guy in the market said a hundred thousand rupiah. I said fifty thousand. And he said one hundred thousand. And I said seventy thousand. And he said one hundred thousand. So, I paid one hundred thousand rupiah.'

There is no doubt that some individuals are instinctively more comfortable than others in negotiating deals. We may safely assume, for instance, that Kiam would have paid less in that Indonesian market than Wang. Some people are just born better at knowing when to push hard, when to give way, when to turn their back and when to sign on the dotted line. But for all that certain people may have an inbuilt advantage, there is still much that an entrepreneur can learn and coach into themselves to ensure that they can negotiate the right deals:

• Lay the groundwork. The most important part of any negotiation takes place before the negotiating parties even get to the point of sitting round a table to hammer out terms. Do your due diligence, finding out everything you can about the other party – look at public records and accounts, speak to third parties who might have worked with them in the past, etc. At the same time, be sure of your own ground. Acknowledge your own side's strengths and weaknesses. In his classic treatise on strategy, *The Art of War*, the ancient philosopher Sun Tzu noted: 'If you know the enemy and know yourself, you need not fear the result of a hundred battles. If you know yourself but not the enemy, for every victory gained you will also suffer a defeat. If you know neither the enemy nor yourself, you will succumb in every battle.'

- Calculate your bottom line. If you go to an auction, it is usually recommended that you figure out the maximum price you are willing to bid and then stick to it, so as not to get caught up in the excitement of the moment. The same rule applies to negotiating a business deal. Know beforehand what the minimum terms are that you can accept. Aim above them but don't accept below them. Warren Buffett has observed that 'price is what you pay, value is what you get'. The numbers in a deal have to represent value to the entrepreneur.

- Get yourself in good shape for the negotiations. Ensure you are well rested and refreshed. Turn up early at the venue so you can prepare yourself and embark on talks on the front foot. If possible, play out possible negotiating scenarios with a friend or colleague in advance. If you appear at the negotiations last minute, dishevelled and bleary-eyed (perhaps from lying awake all night worrying about what is to come), you have already handed an advantage to your counterparts.

- Act in good faith. Each side wants to get the best possible deal for themselves, of course. But negotiations are almost doomed to go wrong if one or both parties enter into them on the defensive, convinced that the other is trying to get one over on them. Listen to the other side's point of view, and they will most likely listen to yours too. Openness is no guarantee that a deal can be struck but it is the most likely path to that holy grail of negotiations, the win–win deal in which everyone feels like they have an agreement that works for them. In her 2009 book, *Making Sense of Business: A No-Nonsense Guide to Business Skills*, Alison Branagan cited the legendary oil tycoon John Paul Getty: 'My father said, "You must never try to make all the money that's in a deal. Let the other fellow make some money too, because if you have a reputation for always making all the money, you won't have many deals."'

- Don't be rushed. Do not allow yourself to be manoeuvred into a position that you're uncomfortable with. In *Company Manners: An Insider Tells How to Succeed in the Real World of Corporate Protocol and Power Politics* (1986), Lois Wyse wrote: 'The single and most dangerous word to be spoken in business is no. The second most dangerous word is yes. It is possible to avoid saying either.'

- Know when to call a halt. If your opposite number refuses to budge on an unacceptable deal, it can feel like a personal affront. But don't get caught up in a squabble. Stay calm and walk away. It was not the right deal, so wait for the one that is. Equally, negotiating can feel like a long game of chess but suddenly you find yourself positioned just as you want to be. Don't let that moment pass but immediately call an end to the game, shake hands and get the contracts drafted.

The entrepreneur can learn much from the skills of those negotiating in fields other than business. For instance, Robert H. Mnookin – a Harvard Law School professor and author of *Bargaining with the Devil: When to Negotiate, When to Fight* – cites South African anti-apartheid leader and the nation's first black president, Nelson Mandela, as the greatest negotiator of the twentieth century. 'He rejected the simple-minded notion,' Mnookin argues, 'that one must either negotiate with the Devil or forcibly resist. He did both. He was willing to make concessions, but not about what was most important to him. With respect to his key political principles, he was unmovable.' In other words, he was willing to be flexible in pursuit of the deal that satisfied his most fundamental (and non-negotiable) aims. Such a strategy will serve any budding entrepreneur well.

Negotiating can feel like a frenzied business, a test of one side's resolve and power against the other side's. The true skill is to make sure that your negotiations are just that – a working-out of terms to everybody's broad satisfaction – and not a confrontation. To achieve this, the entrepreneur must show patience, laying the groundwork, playing fair and knowing what does and does not work for them. Francis Bacon summed it up neatly in his essay of 1597, 'Of Negotiating': 'In all negotiations of difficulty, a man may not look to sow and reap at once; but must prepare business, and so ripen it by degrees.'

THE REAL DEAL

In his 1992 book *Hard Drive*, James Wallace quotes Microsoft's Bill Gates: 'Let's call the real world and try to sell something to it.' It was an aim he fulfilled spectacularly when he signed a deal with computing heavyweights IBM in 1980. IBM was struggling for an operating system for its personal computers and Gates agreed to provide one, although he didn't yet possess it. The result was MS-DOS. Gates's stroke of genius was to sell IBM the operating system for a snip on condition that he retained copyright. His gamble paid off when his operating system came to dominate the personal-computer industry that exploded in the 1980s, earning Microsoft far more than IBM would ever have paid. It was truly the deal of a lifetime.

Be Wily

'How do you beat Bobby Fischer? You play him at
any game but chess. I try to stay in games where I
have an edge.'

WARREN BUFFETT, *BUSINESSWEEK* (1999)

It is possible for a business to offer the best product or service on the market at the fairest price and to strive to give their customers an unrivalled experience, and yet still struggle. Long-term success ultimately relies on how good your offering is, but getting a foothold in the market often requires a number of other factors too. Sheer good luck, for instance – like the umbrella company that opens its doors just as the wet season hits. But another feature of successful entrepreneurism, often less spoken of, is wiliness: the ability to make the shrewd decision at just the right moment to stack the game in your favour.

For instance, elsewhere in this book (see pages 107 and 184), we have seen how the lasting success of Microsoft was founded at least in part on two incredibly wily pieces of business executed by Bill Gates. First, the deal with MITS that promised a BASIC translator that Microsoft had not yet developed, and which Gates could not be entirely sure of their success in doing so. Then, a few years later, the decision not to sell outright to industry leaders IBM an operating system for their personal computers, but instead to license it to them and retain the copyright. Two enormous gambles but ones that paid off handsomely and then some. Gates may have been a relative newcomer to the commercial world but he demonstrated an instinctive shrewdness and an ability to judge when to push in a particular direction.

Jeff Bezos is another case study in wiliness. When he embarked on his Amazon adventure, he dreamed of ultimately creating an 'everything store'. But he knew he had to establish the business a sector at a time. So, he coolly analysed all the commodities he might sell first. The book business, he realized, had done little to embrace the technological revolution represented by the internet. But books lent themselves well to his needs. There is always a large, geographically spread market for them; the books themselves are non-perishable and reasonably easy to store and transport; and each even has its own unique identification number to ensure that orders are reasonably easy to fulfil.

Moreover, the online environment gave rise to the prospect of offering customers a choice of millions of books, while Bezos knew that even the largest physical bookstore could stock at very most 150,000 volumes or so. An online bookstore, then, had an instant competitive advantage. By the time that the US's largest traditional bookstore chain, Barnes &

Noble, got around to selling online, Amazon had already notched up two years of trading. Barnes & Noble never caught up and today Amazon is that 'everything store' Bezos once imagined.

In many cultures, being wily and shrewd is often regarded in a negative light. Those given the label are seen in terms akin to the dreaded cunning fox, that symbol of underhand deviousness. But, in the early twentieth century, Henry Ford's treatment of his workforce demonstrated how it is possible to be at once wily and benevolent. He began paying his employees well above the industry standard in what was regarded by some at the time as an act of commercial suicide. In fact, by being a generous remunerator, he managed to boost his business. His happy workers responded to their better pay by being more productive than virtually all of Ford's rivals, since they wanted to keep their jobs and because they were motivated. Absenteeism reduced dramatically. Moreover, because the desirability of working for Ford meant there wasn't a large staff turnover, the boss had to pay out less to train new employees. And when he did need new workers, the quality of those applying was at a higher level than ever before. The move also served as great PR for the company and there was another advantage too: by developing a loyal, well-paid workforce, he was also nurturing future buyers of his vehicles, as his employees were able to save and join the emerging middle class at whom Ford aimed his cars.

Warren Buffett, heralded as perhaps the leading investment sage of the age, is another who knows more than most about what makes enterprises tick. His quotation at the beginning of this section reinforces the idea that there is nothing underhand about attempting to play the game in the circumstances that give you best advantage. Instead, it is simply good common sense – which is, perhaps, all that shrewdness really is.

Buffett's whole commercial philosophy is based around conducting your business rationally, analytically and to your gain. In 1999 he explained to *Businessweek* how he has always sought to 'control the urges that get other people into trouble in investing' – in other words, to always work in a level-headed way. Then, in 2008, he explained his chief rule of buying to *The New York Times*: 'Be fearful when others are greedy, and be greedy when others are fearful.' Once again, the message is clear: stand back and see where you can exploit a competitive advantage. Don't follow the crowd, or get swept along in its emotions. Focus instead on doing the sensible thing, the prudent thing that everyone else has missed. To do so is not to be underhand or devious. It's just good business.

GREAT DEAL IT IS

George Lucas is responsible for having signed one of the shrewdest deals in movie history. At the time he signed up to produce and direct *Star Wars* in the 1970s, he was on a fee of some $150,000 a movie. He was offered over three times as much for *Star Wars* but decided to strike a different deal instead. He opted to retain his $150,000 pay rate in return for merchandising rights and retaining the rights to any sequels (this at a time when film franchises were far less common than they are today). The executives at 20th Century Fox readily agreed, unaware of what a monster hit the *Star Wars* brand would become. In return for sacrificing his one-time payment, Lucas sealed a bargain that has gone on to net him billions. I sense the shrewdness was strong in this one.

Stick to Your Principles

'The principles we live by, in business and
in social life, are the most important part of
happiness. We need to be careful, upon achieving
happiness, not to lose the virtues which have
produced it.'

HARRY HARRISON, *THE ROTARIAN* (1955)

In 1966, Daniel Katz and Robert L. Kahn wrote in *The Social Psychology of Organizations*: 'It is a commonplace executive observation that businesses exist to make money, and the observation is usually allowed to go unchallenged. It is, however, a very limited statement about the purposes of business.'

Of course, any business must aim to make money. If it consistently fails to do so, it will no longer exist. But now perhaps more than ever, there is increasing pressure for commercial activities to be carried out in an ethical way – the age of all being fair in love, war and business is coming to an end. Of course, that is not to say that many businesses – including some who count among the global giants – don't sometimes have a loose relationship with morality when it comes to the bottom line. Nonetheless, the price to be paid if a firm is exposed as acting unethically can be huge – even existential.

It is said that real integrity is doing the right thing, even when you know that nobody's going to know whether you did it or not.' Doing the right thing in business is not always easy. Doing the wrong thing can sometimes be a lot less hassle. But taking the ethical path is not merely a case of giving yourself a fuzzy feeling inside (although that is one real benefit). Ethics and integrity also make commercial sense.

Firstly, doing the right thing is a sure way to keep out of legal and regulatory bother. Such are the international laws surrounding financial transparency, market competition, customer privacy, environmental responsibility and the like that 'taking shortcuts' in such areas is not a viable option for an enterprise that aspires to long-term success. But being ethical is about much more than merely adhering to the law.

A company with a top-down ethical culture sets the tone for its employees and those it does business with. Paying a fair wage and ensuring equality of opportunity, for instance, are helpful ways to attract and retain the most effective and enterprising workers. And creating an expectation of high ethical standards is reported to encourage staff to make better business choices more quickly. Moreover, a company that plays fair with its commercial partners is far more likely to foster and maintain long-term mutually beneficial relationships than a business that plays fast and loose.

Customers love a 'good' business too. You might think of it as the 'free range' effect. Look at an average supermarket shelf full of eggs and some will be of the factory-farmed variety, selling at a low price. Then there will be the free-range organic ones, selling at a premium price. It takes greater effort and costs more to produce these, but the potential rewards in terms of higher-priced sales make it a stable business model. Similarly, products such as chocolate and coffee have the Fair Trade label (denoting that developing-world producers received a fair price for their produce) that allows sellers to market at a premium price. Recent years have also seen a rapid increase in the number of investors who favour 'ethical investments', so being able to show that you do things the right way can make it easier to access finance. Being ethical, then, really can be good for business and for a company's image.

A case study in how being good can be good for business is The Body Shop, the cosmetics and toiletries giant established by Anita Roddick. A teacher, she spent several years travelling the world and while doing so realized how varied different cultures were in their view of beauty, health and the human body. When she returned home, she felt alienated from the make-up industry in the UK. Companies were in the habit of making big claims for their products but were much vaguer about what went into them.

She decided she wanted to open a make-up and toiletries business that played by a different set of rules. All her products were to be made with natural, ethically sourced ingredients. That meant that the people producing those ingredients, wherever they might be in the world, should have a safe place to work, fair working conditions and a fair wage. She also made her customers part of the ethical story. Utilizing her skills as a teacher, she was an instinctive communicator who gave them the tools to understand where her products came from, how they were produced, how they were tested and what they could do for the consumer. Her honesty allowed her clientele to feel that they were not merely buying some bubble bath but were more intimately invested in the business.

She opened her first shop in 1976 and a second followed within the year. By 1982, there was an average of two new shops opening every month. Roddick spent virtually nothing on formal marketing but achieved this impressive growth thanks to word-of-mouth recommendations. Her customers loved her products and her ethos, and were delighted to share the secret with all their friends too. Here was ethical conduct as a driver of the bottom line.

Roddick stayed committed to her founding principles as the profits poured in. She was, for instance, a powerful advocate for environmental causes and was a noted supporter of Amnesty International. She also spearheaded a campaign against animal testing, which was a standard part of the production process for most of her large-scale business rivals. Her message was simple: it was cruel to expose animals to often painful and distressing testing in the name of beauty. She proved that you could run a business in that field without resorting to doing that. Such campaigning zeal served to maintain the business's sense of humanity even as it rapidly expanded. Customers felt they were not only buying a product but were also buying *into* a culture, into values. They felt a connection to the brand and its figurehead that nurtured extraordinary customer loyalty. When she finally sold the company in 2006 to focus on other interests, it boasted more than 2,000 stores in over fifty countries, catering to nearly 80 million customers, and was valued at £650 million.

Ethics and profits, she conclusively proved, need not be mutually exclusive. In fact, the former can boost the latter. As she told *Inc.* magazine in 1990:

I believe quite passionately that there is a better way. I think you can rewrite the book on business. I think you can trade ethically; be committed to social responsibility, global responsibility; empower your employees without being afraid of them. I think you can really rewrite the book. That is the vision, and the vision is absolutely clear.

WHAT'S IN A NAME?

When Anita Roddick opened her first store, in Brighton on the south coast of England, there were one or two dissenting voices. In particular, she upset the business next door – but not because they were competing in the same market. They were a firm of funeral directors and they were not at all comfortable that the neighbours were operating under the name of The Body Shop! The ever-sharp Roddick spotted an opportunity, however, and made sure to tell the local papers of the disagreement. Sure enough, the free publicity drove new customers to her shop.

Money is Not the Only Marker of Success

'It's a common misconception that money is every
entrepreneur's metric for success. It's not, and nor
should it be.'

RICHARD BRANSON, LINKEDIN ARTICLE (2016)

Successful entrepreneurship and making money naturally go hand in hand. No one wins a business award for racking up the biggest losses on the bottom line. As Elon Musk told the Inc. 5000 Conference in 2008: 'Fundamentally, if you don't have a compelling product at a compelling price, you don't have a great company.' Yet, for all that, it is noticeable how often business titans suggest that financial success is often overrated as a measure of how well an entrepreneur is doing.

In the article quoted at the start of this section, Branson went on to argue: 'Too many people measure how successful they are by how much money they make or the people that they associate with. In my opinion, true success should be measured by how happy you are.' Some people might have a knee-jerk response here, along the lines that such sentiments are easy to hold when you've got a few billion in the bank. Money may not be able to buy you happiness, it has been said, but it can buy you a far more comfortable standard of misery. Yet Branson is adamant that more important to him than the bottom line is the sense that his businesses have 'made a positive difference in people's lives'. It is from this starting point – a wish to make a difference – he says, that his companies then make money: because they are meeting their aims of providing people with what they want and need. Similarly, on a personal level, he has said: 'Most people would assume my business success, and the wealth that comes with it, have brought me happiness. But I know I am successful, wealthy and connected because I am happy.'

Nor is Branson alone in his outlook. Warren Buffett, for example, told students at the University of Nebraska–Lincoln in 1994: 'It's a little crazy, it seems to me, if you are building a business and creating a business, not to create something you are going to enjoy when you get through. It's like painting a painting. I mean, you ought to paint something you are going to enjoy looking at when you get through.' In other words, what is the point of being an entrepreneur if your business is only about making money and not about bringing satisfaction? Similarly, Oprah Winfrey told the Academy of Achievement in 1991:

What others view as successful is not my idea of what success is. And I don't mean to belittle it at all. It's really nice to be able to have nice things. What material success does is provide you with the ability to concentrate on other things that really matter. And that is being able to make a difference, not only in your own life, but in other people's lives.

That is why there are many truly successful entrepreneurs who will never appear on *Fortune*'s list of the world's richest. A business need not be vast to provide an entrepreneur with a reasonable level of income and a sense of profound personal satisfaction. If your business provides you with, perhaps, sufficient finances for the lifestyle you want (there is nothing to say that an entrepreneur must yearn for a personal jet or private yacht rather than, say, an ordinary car), if you broadly enjoy your work and have the resources to indulge some of your personal passions, then your entrepreneurial adventure must surely be judged more successful than the miserable billionaire checking his bank balance in his lonely castle.

This trend towards re-evaluating how we measure success extends beyond just the commercial world. In recent years, many academics have suggested that Gross Domestic Product (GDP – the sum total of what a country produces in a year, or, to put it another way, a country's bottom line) is a deeply flawed measure of a nation's success. Since the early 1970s, the small Himalayan state of Bhutan has operated a 'Gross National Happiness' index instead.

Meanwhile, a growing body of economists now question whether the pursuit of constant economic growth is either achievable or desirable. The success of large numbers of social enterprises in recent years further goes to prove that certain companies lead the way in improving the world and giving satisfaction to their customers and employees even if they largely fail to register the ginormous profits of, for example, the giants of Silicon Valley.

In practical terms, there are several measures unrelated to profit (and beyond even their own personal contentedness) by which an entrepreneur may judge the success of their company. These might include:

- Are your customers satisfied? Even if the company is not making a fortune, is it retaining or even growing its customer base? If you can attract customers and provide them with a service that gives them satisfaction, then long-term financial viability is highly probable too.
- Are your workforce onside? A business in trouble rarely manages to conceal its problems from those working at the coalface. But contented employees are often a sign of a business on the right tracks.
- How are your competitors doing? If you are going through a tough time, it may be that the whole market is. Even if your bottom-line profits are declining, do you retain a stable market share? Is

it possible that you are staying ahead of the curve even as you struggle? As long as your specific sector is not in terminal decline, such a scenario suggests healthy future prospects.

It would be obtuse to suggest that making money is not a vital aspect of the entrepreneurial experience. Failure to keep the cash flow ticking over and the bank manager happy usually results in the end of the entrepreneurial dream. But the unquestioning association of business success with core financials gives at best an incomplete picture of how well an enterprise is operating. You, your employees and your customers should all be drawing satisfaction from your business in ways that cannot be measured in simply financial terms.

Running a business is not meant to be a non-stop party. As Elon Musk said during his Khan Academy Chat in 2013: 'A lot of times people think creating companies is going to be fun. I would say it's not. It's really not that fun. There are periods of fun, and there are periods where it's just awful.' But he also acknowledges that maintaining your original passion makes the task far less awful, as when he noted at Tesla's 2016 Annual Shareholder Meeting: 'It's just so much easier to work hard if you love what you're doing.' It was a desire to maintain those feelings of 'first love' that persuaded Mark Zuckerberg to turn down Yahoo's offer of a billion dollars for Facebook back in 2006, at a time when it was not certain that such money would be on offer again. 'I don't know what I could do with the money,' he figured. 'I'd just start another social-networking site. I kind of like the one I already have.'

Jeff Bezos echoes the notion of staying rooted to the 'inner you', telling Four Peaks TV in 2013: 'It's a gift if you can keep your childlike sense of wonder, and it helps with creativity. It helps to have fun.' He is also someone who suggests that good stewardship is encouraged by actively seeking connection with those at the coalface, where the entrepreneur themselves likely started. In 2003 he observed in *Fortune*: 'I've not seen an effective manager or leader who can't spend some fraction of time down in the trenches. If they can't do that, they get out of touch with reality, and their whole thought and management process becomes abstracted and disconnected.'

In the interests of overall contentedness, then, being boss of your own enterprise should be more than just about your profit-and-loss column. As Branson observed, entrepreneurial success and personal happiness feed into one another. That is why it is vital to keep an eye on the non-financial measures of your business. Heed the words of Warren Buffett to the *Georgia Tech Alumni Magazine* in 2003: 'You gotta do what you love. You've got to have a passion for it. If you're not doing it, get into something else.'

WAYNE'S WORLD

Ronald Wayne is not a household name but he is proof that there is much more to life than money. He'd met Steve Jobs and Steve Wozniak when he was an engineer at Atari, and the Steves later brought him on board when they founded Apple. He was to provide the fledgling company with some supervision (he was in his forties while they were in their twenties) and he would write the company's original partnership agreement, which granted him a 10 per cent stake in Apple. But he soon realized that the job was not for him; he lasted less than two weeks before cashing in his shares for $800 and finding work at a small engineering firm. Today his 10 per cent would be worth tens of billions of dollars but back in 2014 Wayne told the Cult of Mac website that he had no regrets about the path he followed, which cost him a fortune. 'If I had stayed with Apple,' he reflected, 'I probably would have wound up the richest man in the cemetery.'

Perhaps we should all ultimately be aiming for the sort of vision that liquor-business veteran and communications specialist Gary Vaynerchuk expressed in his book *Crush It!* (2009):

Live your passion. What does that mean, anyway? It means that when you get up for work every morning, every single morning, you are pumped because you get to talk about or work with or do the thing that interests you the most in the world. You don't live for vacations because you don't need a break from what you're doing – working, playing, and relaxing are one and the same. You don't even pay attention to how many hours you're working because to you, it's not really work. You're making money, but you'd do whatever it is you're doing for free.'

Share the Wealth

'Thus is the problem of Rich and Poor to be solved. The laws of accumulation will be left free; the laws of distribution free. Individualism will continue, but the millionaire will be but a trustee of the poor; entrusted for a season with a great part of the increased wealth of the community, but administering it for the community far better than it could or would have done for itself.'

ANDREW CARNEGIE, 'WEALTH', IN

NORTH AMERICAN REVIEW (1889)

As we saw in the last chapter, success for many entrepreneurs is as much about 'making a dent in the universe' (as Steve Jobs memorably put it) as it is about making piles of money. One method by which an increasing number of the most successful entrepreneurs make their dent is through philanthropy – a sector that has undergone a significant transformation in the twenty-first century.

George Soros, who made his billions as an investor, has been at the forefront of the modern philanthropic movement, disseminating well over $30 billion of his personal fortune via his Open Society Foundation that supports civil-society groups globally. In 2000 he explained to George Shapiro why he had chosen to spend a large part of his wealth on philanthropic causes:

> It's more difficult, you know, to bring about positive change than it is to make money. It's much easier to make money, because it's a much easier way to measure success – the bottom line. When it comes

to social consequences, they've got all different people acting in different ways, very difficult to even have a proper criterion of success. So, it's a difficult task. Why not use an entrepreneurial, rather than a bureaucratic, approach. As long as people genuinely care for the people they're trying to help, they can actually do a lot of good.

So, just what do we mean by philanthropy? How does it differ from simple charity? Charity is traditionally associated with using resources to address the symptoms of a problem. If someone is hungry, give them a meal. Philanthropy, on the other hand, tends to aim at getting to grips with the root cause of a problem. In the classic example, rather than give the hungry individual a fish to eat, teach them how to fish so that they might provide a meal for themselves, their family and their community – not just today but into the future too. Philanthropy is morally neither better nor worse than charity but in bold economic terms it tends to work at a bigger scale – in terms of both resources inputted and effects outputted. Moreover, where a philanthropist gifts to a charity, by dint of contributing a generally larger amount than the average they tend to have a greater say in how that money is used. It is a fact that undoubtedly appeals to many rich entrepreneurs who are used to overseeing the allocation of large-scale resources in their commercial lives.

Philanthropy is by no means an exclusively modern phenomenon. We can go back to at least the eighteenth century to see how civic organizations sought to administer large-scale schemes to the benefit of those in need. The late nineteenth century proved to be something of a golden age when a wave of hugely rich entrepreneurs, particularly in the USA and UK, used their wealth for philanthropic purposes. Their names – Andrew Carnegie, George Peabody, John D. Rockefeller, Joseph Rowntree and Henry Wellcome among them – live on today.

Now as then, there are three principal models for the philanthropist to follow:

- Making large individual donations to already established organizations.
- Establishing an endowment – a financial gift to a charity or non-profit organization for a particular use (for example, a scholarship). Often, an endowment sustains itself by using monies generated by investing the initial gift.
- Establishing a foundation in their own name aimed at fulfilling specific goals.

Silicon Valley has proved the spiritual home of the new golden age of philanthropy, with Bill Gates perhaps the most famous of them all. It is an accolade that for a long time seemed unlikely. In the 1980s and early

1990s he informed journalists that his attention was focused on growing his business rather than getting involved in more outward-looking projects. But in 1994 he founded the William H. Gates Foundation and a year later wrote in the *New York Times* of the challenges facing the modern philanthropist. 'Spending money intelligently is as difficult as earning it,' he noted. 'Giving away money in meaningful ways will be a main preoccupation later in my life – assuming I still have a lot to give away.' The following year in the same paper he pledged: 'Eventually I'll return most of [my money] as contributions to causes I believe in, such as education and population stability.'

In 1997, he truly announced his arrival as a philanthropic heavyweight when the Gates Library Foundation provided around $400 million in finance and Microsoft software to public libraries, a contribution that outdid what the federal government provided that year. Then, in 2000, he amalgamated all his philanthropic interests into the Bill & Melinda Gates Foundation, which by the end of 2018 had made grants worth over $50 billion in over 130 countries around the world. It is generally thought to be the largest such organization in existence. 'While the private sector does a phenomenal job meeting human needs among those who can pay,' he told *Forbes* in 2012, 'there are billions of people who have no way to express their needs in ways that matter to markets. And so they go without.'

The Gates Foundation has received support totalling many billions from an endowment gifted by Warren Buffett, who has also served as a philanthropy mentor to Gates. Buffett has spoken of his sense of having won the 'ovarian lottery' by being born in the right place (the USA) and at the right time in history so that his ability to allocate capital (which is how he sees the role of the investor) earned him a fortune. This has driven his subsequent desire to give something back. As he told *Fortune* in 2006:

> Andrew Carnegie […] said that huge fortunes that flow in large part from society should in large part be returned to society. In my case, the ability to allocate capital would have had little utility unless I lived in a rich, populous country in which enormous quantities of marketable securities were traded and were sometimes ridiculously mispriced. And fortunately for me, that describes the United States in the second half of the last century.

On key fundamentals, he believes that business and philanthropy are in key respects fundamentally at odds with each other. In 2011 he told the newspaper *Haaretz*: 'In business you are looking for easy problems. In philanthropy you are looking for very tough problems. If you are doing serious, big philanthropy, you are looking at problems that defied intellect for a long time and people have known they were important. So, you've got to expect way more failure.'

It is a lesson that the Gates Foundation has taken to heart as it tailors its missions for both the particular needs of the USA (where it seeks to expand educational opportunities and access to information technology) and those of the international community (for whom its goals are enhanced healthcare and a reduction in extreme poverty). Globally, it has invested billions into the fight against diseases such as AIDS, tuberculosis and malaria, all of which are far more prevalent in developing nations. There have also been ambitious goals set to eradicate polio from the planet and to redesign a new type of flushing toilet to improve the lives of some 4.5 billion people who live without access to safe sanitation.

The mega-rich entrepreneurs created out of the technological revolution have undeniably changed the face of philanthropy. Their vast resources have made it possible to tackle problems that hitherto had been beyond the scope of charities and even governments. But it is possible to be philanthropic on a smaller budget. Like running a business, it is essentially about the wise allocation of resources. A donation of a few thousand won't, say, fund all the research necessary to cure cancer, but it might perhaps pay for an endowment that pays the scholarship for the doctor who goes on to help find the cure. For those who feel that they have been well rewarded in their commercial lives, it is undoubtedly a valuable and personally rewarding means to 'balance the books' by contributing to the greater good. As Gates put it to journalists in 2006:

I believe that with great wealth comes great responsibility, a responsibility to give back to society, a responsibility to see that those resources are put to work in the best possible way to help those most in need.

THE BILLIONAIRES CLUB

The Gateses (Bill and Melinda) and Buffett are behind one of the most extraordinary developments in modern philanthropy – the Giving Pledge campaign. Since 2010 it has targeting billionaires (or people who would be billionaires were it not for their existing charitable giving), urging them to agree to give away 50 per cent or more of their wealth to good causes. As of 2019, there were over 200 signatories to the pledge, which in time should ensure the philanthropic sector is flooded with a quantity of money that makes even the Bill & Melinda Gates Foundation's contribution seem moderate.

Social Entrepreneurship: Philanthropy+

'I'm encouraging young people to become social business entrepreneurs and contribute to the world, rather than just making money. Making money is no fun. Contributing to and changing the world is a lot more fun.'

MUHAMMAD YUNUS, FOUNDER OF GRAMEEN BANK, GLOBAL SOCIAL SUMMIT, 2010

Philanthropy is a long-established and highly frutiful method by which the entrepreneur can use their business acumen to do good in the world. But it is only one model. For some entrepreneurs with an eye on social responsibility, the approach can seem disjointed. Philanthropy requires the initial accumulation of wealth by traditional commercial routes, and then a secondary process of disseminating that wealth. But what if you can be 'doing good' at the very same time as doing business? This is where social entrepreneurism comes in – a phenomenon that has come on in leaps and bounds in recent decades.

Any successful business, as we have seen, must identify a market need and then provide the means to meet that need. The social entrepreneur begins by identifying a social need, then designing a business that meets the need and which adopts the same sustainable business structures as any other commercial enterprise. In other words, a social enterprise does not seek to do its work by relying on voluntary donations (as, say, a charity would) but by establishing a commercial model whereby it generates sufficient revenues itself to continue its work. It may be that a social enterprise runs certain programmes that are not themselves commercially viable, but the cost of these must be absorbed by other parts of the business that are. In *Social Entrepreneurship: The Art of Mission-Based Venture Development*, Peter C. Brinckerhoff described the social entrepreneur like this:

> To me the core of social entrepreneurship is good stewardship. Good stewards don't rest on their laurels, they try new things, serve people in new ways, are lifelong learners, try to have their organizations be fonts of excellence [...] They weigh the social and financial return of each of their investments.

Social enterprises take a vast array of forms. Some employ people with disabilities to provide a working wage that may otherwise not be available to them. Some, like TOMS (see box at the end of chapter) run commercial and social programmes in tandem, while others provide social services on a commercial footing. Bill Drayton, the founder of Ashoka – an organization that looks to foster social enterprises around the world – has given a sense of how social entrepreneurs look to shake up established ways of doing business. They are, he says, 'not content just to give a fish or teach how to fish. They will not rest until they have revolutionized the fishing industry.'

Jean Bosco Nzeyimana offers a case study in how a social entrepreneur can work to solve several problems in one go. He grew up in rural Rwanda, with his early life marked by deprivation. His village had no electricity and his journey to school each day included a detour through the woods to find firewood, a sometimes perilous task that left him exhausted before the school day had even begun. Moreover, he knew that the felling of trees for fuel was having a detrimental environmental impact on the local area, causing erosion that created huge gullies routinely used for landfill.

The village seemed caught in a catch-22 of environmental degradation, but then Nzeyimana had the idea to turn the area's organic waste into clean-burning briquettes that could be used both as fuel and as fertilizer for crops. In 2013 he set up an enterprise called Habona (meaning 'Illumination'), which worked with both the local authorities and international technical partners to turn his idea into reality. He started collecting waste to make the biofuel that in turn has reduced the need for further deforestation, putting less strain on the land and cutting the volume of waste-dumping, as well as saving many villagers from the arduous job of collecting wood. A year after setting up business – providing paid work to local citizens – he was awarded the African Innovation Prize and hopes to extend his winning formula into many other areas in the years to come.

One of the key figures in expanding the social-entrepreneurship movement back in the 1970s was Muhammad Yunus, the Bangladeshi founder of the Grameen Bank. In 2006 he and his organization were jointly awarded the Nobel Peace Prize for 'their efforts through microcredit to create economic and social development from below'. Two years later, *Foreign Policy* magazine rated him second in their list of the 'Top 100 Global Thinkers'.

At the heart of Yunus's philosophy of social entrepreneurship is the recognition that millions of people around the world are trapped in poverty because they cannot access finance. As he told PBS in 2016: 'I said, "All human beings are born entrepreneurs. Some get a chance to unleash that capacity. Some never got the chance, never knew that he or she has that capacity."' In 1976, Yunus came up with a potential solution to this inequality. He founded a bank to focus on providing microcredit to those in need of it – a strategy that has gained momentum in the years since so that microfinancing has become a significant weapon in the global war against poverty.

In 1976, the Grameen Bank loaned a group of Bangladeshi women $27. With this money, they were able to buy the materials they needed (but could not themselves afford) so that they could use their craft skills to manufacture bamboo stools, which they then sold. As individuals, the women would likely not have qualified for credit from a traditional bank, which may well have demanded some form of collateral too. But the Grameen Bank was content to provide the money, aware of the likelihood that the women would generate sufficient revenue to pay it back in full over a reasonable timescale. Moreover, such was the scale of the loan that, should the women's enterprise fail, non-payment would not be overly damaging to the bank. As events played out, the women did fulfil repayment and created a sustainable business that would otherwise have been beyond their grasp.

Microloans are, as their name suggests, routinely small, from as little as $10 and rarely more than a few thousand. They are often given to groups, too, which tend to self-regulate and ensure that each member of the collective is encouraged to put maximum effort into achieving each individual business's success. The Grameen Bank paved the way for a micro-financing revolution as it became evident that large numbers of people could be lifted out of poverty by a mechanism that was commercially viable to all involved (microfinancing institutions generally accepting that their profits are unlikely to rival those in the more cut-throat commercial end of banking) and which, crucially, did not demand government intervention. Indeed, in his 2001 autobiography, *Banker to the Poor*, Yunus wrote:

> I believe that 'government', as we know it today, should pull out of most things except for law enforcement and justice, national defence and foreign policy, and let the private sector, a 'Grameenized private sector', a social-consciousness-driven private sector, take over their other functions.

Such a view may be unrealistic and, perhaps, even undesirable, but it goes to show how Yunus and social entrepreneurs like him have turned traditional notions of entrepreneurship upside down. Social entrepreneurism allows its exponents to not only explore the traditional challenges of entrepreneurism – to meet a need in a commercially viable way – but also enact lasting change in the world. While it *is* possible to make a personal fortune in the world of social entrepreneurship, it is less easy than in the more traditional field of purely commercial entrepreneurism. But for those individuals who believe that their success can be evidenced by factors other than the vastness of their bank balance, social entrepreneurship offers the potential to have the best of all worlds and make the best world they can for others too.

ONE STEP AT A TIME

In 2006, an American named Blake Mycoskie founded a shoe company called Toms. Inspired by his travels in Argentina, he developed designs for alpargatas (canvas slip-on shoes popular in Argentina) to sell into the North American market. But Toms was a social enterprise and its unique selling point was that the company would provide a free pair of shoes to a young person in need in Argentina (as well as other developing nations) for each pair sold in North America. Mycoskie termed this the 'One for One' model and it proved a highly effective strategy, especially when the company also moved a large part of its production to developing countries.